Foster Care Matters

Foster Care Matters

Edited by
Elizabeth Harlow

W&B

MMXI

Chapters 4, 5, 7 and 9 of this book first appeared in *Social Work & Social Sciences Review* volume 13(1). Chapters 3, 6, 8 and 10 first appeared in *Social Work & Social Sciences Review* volume 13(2)

© Whiting & Birch Ltd 2011
Published by Whiting & Birch Ltd,
Forest Hill, London SE23 3HZ

ISBN 9781861771179

Printed in England, Austalia and the United States by Lightning Source

Contents

About the authors

Foluke Blackburn Associate Director of Social Work, University of Salford.
f.blackburn@salford.ac.uk

Bob Broad is Professor of Children and Families Research, London South
Bank University. broadb@lsbu.ac.uk

Jo Dixon is a Research Fellow, Social Policy Researcg Unit, University of
York. jd21@york.ac.uk

Elaine Farmer is Professor of Child and Family Studies, School for Policy
Studies, University of Bristol. e.r.farmer@bristol.ac.uk

Nick Frost is Professor of Social Work (Children, Childhood & Families),
Leeds Metropolitan University. n.frost@leedsmet.ac.uk

Elizabeth Harlow is Professor of Social Work, Faculty of Health and Social
Care, University of Chester. e.harlow@chester.ac.uk

Derek Kirton is Reader in Social Policy and Social Work, School of Social
Policy, Sociology and Social Research, The University of Kent, Canterbury.
D.Kirton@kent.ac.uk

Jo Lipscombe is Research Fellow, School for Policy Studies, University of
Bristol. Jo.Lipscombe@bristol.ac.uk

Janette Logan is Senior Lecturer in Social Work, University of Manchester.
Janette.Logan@manchester.ac.uk

Clive Sellick is Reader in Social Work and Psychology, University of East Anglia.
c.sellick@uea.ac.uk

Carole Smith Honorary Senior Lecturer, School of Nursing, Midwifery and
Social Work University of Manchester. crsmith@manchester.ac.uk

1
Introduction

Elizabeth Harlow

In the autumn of 2006, in response to growing concern that the care system was failing children, the government of the United Kingdom introduced its Green Paper *Care Matters: Transforming the Lives of Children and Young People in Care* (DfES 2006). The reform agenda included: the responsibilities of the corporate parent; the education of young people in care; life outside of education; the transition to adulthood; the multi-professional prevention of care; and the performance of the care system itself. The consultation associated with the launch of the Green Paper intended to encourage a 'national debate on the future of care' and it was against this backdrop that a symposium on foster care was organised by the editor of this volume with funding from the publishers Whiting and Birch and the national charity the Fostering Network[1].

The event (Fostering Matters: A Symposium Focussing on the Future of Foster Care) which took place on 28th March 2007 at the University of Salford, was attended by policy makers, the senior managers of children's services, as well as leading academics. Based on empirical research and theoretical developments, the papers presented offered an academic perspective and articulated the drivers behind the Green Paper referenced above, but also the subsequent White Paper (DfES 2007). Some of these and other compatible contributions have been published as two volumes of a special edition of the journal *Social Work and Social Sciences Review*. By including these papers (together with two additional chapters that have been provided by Carole Smith), this book showcases knowledge that is influencing the future of foster care, but also offers critical comment on government policy. Policy context and detail are the primary focus of chapters two to seven, although chapter six is a critical reflection on policy trends and policy implementation. Chapters eight, nine and ten are more concerned with practice. Finally, in chapter eleven, the main themes of the symposium are drawn together and Smith, in putting the needs of children and young people to the fore, offers her own overarching comment. What follows here is a brief outline of each of the forthcoming chapters.

Chapter two. Foster care in context: From waiting in the wings to centre stage Carole Smith

By taking a chronological approach, Smith narrates the development of foster care from its informal and unregulated origins in the sixteenth century. When parents have been in need or in such distress that they have been unable to provide (physically and/or emotionally) for their children, then a range of alternative solutions have been made available by charities or the state. Over recent times, substitute family care has been seen as preferable to residential options, as has the speedy return of children to their families of origin. Smith locates this development within its empirical context and in so doing also acknowledges the influence of the American permanence movement, and its impact on adoption as well as fostering policies. More recently, research conducted in the UK has focussed on the experiences of young people who have been looked after as they make their transition to adulthood. The reduced life chances of these young people highlight the struggle in making this transition, but also the inadequacy of their formative care. Smith describes the range of polices deployed by the UK government in its attempt to improve the quality of care in general and in particular the preparation of young people for adulthood. All of this has led to the spotlight finally being shone on the practice of foster care. As Smith says:

> There is a demonstrable relationship between stable placements, children's experience of security and permanence and their educational achievement and social wellbeing. It is not surprising therefore, that foster care must play a significant role in helping to improve the life chances of looked after children and young people (p. 16).

Within the context of its policy and practice history, Smith sets the scene for the current emphasis on the recruitment, training, support and remuneration of foster care. In so doing, Smith makes an important contribution to the framing of the forthcoming chapters.

Chapter three. Reforming the care system: New Labour and corporate parenting Elizabeth Harlow and Nick Frost

Chapter three is a development of the scene setting presentation made by Nick Frost, professor of Social Work (Children, Childhood and Families), at the symposium. In this chapter Harlow and Frost focus attention on the government as corporate parent to children who are unable to live with their birth parents. It is acknowledged that, irrespective of the good intentions of policy makers, placement providers and professionals, these children have not always been given the care and help adequate to their needs. Although New Labour has already invested in improving the quality of care in a variety of ways, it is the Care Matters policy initiative that explicitly identifies responsibilities in terms of corporate parenting:

The State has a unique responsibility for children in care. It has taken on the task of parenting some of society's most vulnerable children and in doing so it must become everything a good parent should be. (DfES, 2006, 1.1)

A good corporate parent must offer everything that a good parent would provide and more, addressing both the difficulties which the children experience and the challenges of parenting within a complex system of services (DfES, 2007, 1.20).

This chapter describes and offers critical reflection on proposals for improving a) the educational achievement of young people and b) their relational continuity with social workers. With reference to New Labour's commitment to the 'social investment state' (Giddens, 1998, cited in Fawcett *et al.*, 2004), Harlow and Frost argue that improving corporate parenting is the government's attempt to facilitate young people into becoming included, as opposed to dependent and excluded, adult members of society. Whilst the government's approach may have economic rather than purely altruistic foundations, it is argued that the proposed changes constitute an improvement on the minimalist and stigmatising provision of the past.

Chapter four. Towards a mixed economy of foster care provision
Clive Sellick

Training and financial support for foster carers are important themes within Sellick's chapter, which describes the increasingly mixed market of placement provision and the rising number of Independent Fostering Providers (IFPs). In the past, it was assumed that foster families would be recruited, assessed and supported by the Social Services Departments of Local Authorities. When the Conservatives took office in the 1970s, their commitment to market-based provision of welfare meant that this assumption would be questioned. Despite the political change in 1997 when the New Labour Government was elected, policies have continued to encourage the independent provision of foster care. Now, approximately twenty per cent of all looked after children are placed with foster carers who are trained and supported (financially and in other ways) by IFPs.

Ideologically, markets are expected to drive up standards. From the perspective of foster carers this appears to have happened. IFPs have offered their foster carers a higher level of support than they would have received from the Local Authority, including the payment of substantially higher allowances and in some cases fees. In many regions this has forced Local Authorities to reconsider their approach to their own foster carers in order that they should not be 'poached'. In consequence, it appears that the introduction of the market in foster care provision and the arrival of IFPs, has contributed significantly to the professionalisation of the service.

Chapter five. Step forward? Step back? The professionalisation of fostering Derek Kirton

The professionalisation of foster care has become a major trend over recent times. Derek Kirton elucidates the way in which the increasing demands placed on foster carers has led to calls for their training, substantially increased allowances and in some cases the payment of fees. However, these calls have been countered by others who cherish the ideal of fostering as a voluntary role, carried out within the family for love rather than money. Kirton questions whether love and family really co-exist in opposition to work and money, as suggested by the critics of the trend. He concludes that, although there is no evidence that the professionalisation of foster care improves outcomes for children, on the grounds of social justice and gender equality, it may be a necessary development. Given that the White Paper (DfES 2007) identifies foster carers as members of the child care workforce, this development appears to have become established.

Chapter six. A foster carer's perspective Elizabeth Harlow and Foluke Blackburn

Foluke Blackburn was invited to attend the 'Fostering Matters' symposium not only on the grounds of being a foster carer, but also of being a trainer of foster carers, an experienced social work practitioner and currently a Lecturer in Social Work. Here, Blackburn offers a foster carer's perspective on the *Care Matters* agenda and in a more limited way the symposium itself. The main theme of her deliberation is the professionalisation of foster care. Referring to her own experiences, Blackburn reflects with some ambivalence on this current trend (see Kirton 2007). In addition, approaches to the assessment and training of foster carers are also considered. Although it is appreciated that the opinion of foster carers will vary in relation to their social characteristics, their personal biographies and the context in which their opinions are elicited, it is hoped that this paper will provide insights that have value for all those charged with the responsibility of developing and improving services in this field.

Chapter seven. Kinship care: what works? Who cares? Bob Broad

Broad's chapter shows that questions concerning financial and day-to-day support are also pertinent to the provision of kinship care. Legally acknowledged in the Children Act (1989), and endorsed further in the Green and White papers, kinship care is an increasingly popular option for children who are unable to remain with their birth parents (see below). According to Farmer and Moyers (2006 cited by Broad), the majority of the people providing this kind of care are the child's grandparents. Research indicates that grandparents (and other kinship carers) often struggle with their role, a struggle that results frequently from complicated family dynamics. Despite this struggle, the strength of commitment to the child usually means that the arrangement lasts. In consequence, kinship care is a relatively stable placement option. Not only this, the Local Authority benefits in that the children in need of help are diverted from more costly fostering and residential services. Put another way, grandparents might care for a child at their own expense, whilst foster carers who are 'strangers' would, at a minimal, be provided with an allowance as well as on-going support.

According to Broad, this situation has been described as inequitable by Justice Munby who, with reference to the *European Convention on Human Rights*, ruled that Local Authorities should make payments to carers on the basis of the child's needs, irrespective of whether their relationship was based on a blood tie. Broad is supportive of this stance and, although positive about the increased appreciation of kinship care, indicates in his paper that current policy developments do not go far enough. Whilst suggesting that training for kinship care may not be appropriate, the provision of financial and other supportive resources should occur.

Chapter eight. Lesbian and gay fostering and adoption in the United Kingdom Janette Logan and Clive Sellick

Logan and Sellick do not discuss the government's *Care Matters* agenda directly. Instead, they draw attention to the ongoing and important (though often neglected) topic of foster care and sexuality. Over recent years the social climate has evolved and the currently liberal culture enables lesbians and gay men to adopt and foster children. However, the authors of the paper play with paradox by arguing that although legislation and policy has introduced greater equality, prejudice continues. This means that lesbians and gay men may still feel socially excluded and ostracised. Whilst this has numerous implications for fostering, the authors focus on the potential vulnerabilities of young people and the need for sensitivity if they identify themselves as lesbian or gay. The second issue discussed by Logan and Sellick concerns the assessment of lesbian and gay foster carers. Although the potential contribution of lesbian and gay foster carers has been officially accepted, the criteria by which they are assessed may not have been discussed. With the dominance of the heterosexual family form, Foster Placement Workers or Supervising Social Workers may feel uncertain of how to proceed.

Chapter nine. What matters in fostering adolescents? Jo Lipscombe and Elaine Farmer

Lipscombe and Farmer are committed to the training of all foster carers. Although both the Green and White Papers propose a tiered system in which trained, specialist foster carers will offer placements to the children demonstrating the greatest emotional and behavioural demands, Lipscombe and Farmer argue that 'mainstream' foster carers may also benefit from training in that they also have to care for children with extremely complex needs. This is particularly the case when caring for adolescents whose physical and psychological stage of development, coupled with their familial and social history, can require a high degree of understanding and an insightful, sensitive response. Lipscombe and Farmer reach this conclusion on the basis of empirical evidence emanating from a project funded by the Department of Health (Farmer *et al.* 2004). This research, which is outlined more fully on pp. 111-112 , explored foster carers' parenting strategies and supports in relation to the outcomes of placements for adolescents. The findings indicate that outcomes might be improved if all foster parents are trained to:

> respond to young people's emotional and developmental age; talk to young people about the past and about difficulties in their relationships with their families; monitor adolescents' activities outside the home ... ; and assist young people to develop independence and autonomy whilst also providing them with a secure base' (p.122).

This chapter, therefore, continues the theme of professionalisation, but applies the principles of training to the particular needs of adolescents.

Chapter ten. Obstacles to participation in education, employment and training for young people leaving care Jo Dixon

This chapter reports on an empirical project carried out in the UK between 2001 and 2003 which aimed to explore the early career progress of young people leaving care. It provides evidence for the argument made in chapter three by Harlow and Frost: that is, the recent policy focus has not enabled care leavers to actively engage in education, employment or training (EET) as actively as the wider population (Dixon *et al.*, 2006). Although some progress appears to have been made, it has nevertheless been disappointingly slow. Like Stein (2006), Dixon also points out that the obstacles to participating in EET can occur prior to the young person's admission to care. For example, before becoming accommodated a child may experience loss or trauma, poor parenting, family problems, and socio-economic disadvantage, all of which might have long term negative implications. Dixon traces the problems that might occur whilst a child is looked after: placements may break down which disrupt home life and school attendance. There is a reduced likelihood of participating in EET if whilst in care, young people commit criminal offences and misuse drugs and alcohol. When exploring the obstacles encountered post-care, Dixon structures her discussion by means of the typology generated by the Work Foundation. That is, obstacles may be: personal; institutional; local or structural. Finally, Dixon suggests some policy and practice changes that might help young care leavers avoid a future of unemployment.

Chapter eleven Carers and looked after children: the challenges ahead
Carole Smith

In this concluding chapter Smith integrates and comments upon the themes that have dominated the content of this book. After describing the government's policy as set out in the Green (DfES 2006) and White Papers (DfES 2007), Smith connects the policy to the research findings and theoretical arguments articulated within the presentations made at the symposium. By taking this approach the evidence that is informing the policy is highlighted, but also questions are raised and the potential limitations are thrown into sharp relief. Most importantly, Smith offers her own critique and she takes issue with the government's attempts to improve the lot of looked after children and young people by means of performance indicators, outcome targets and the re-configuration of the system of service provision. The government's inherently contradictory stance to service systems is featured as Smith critiques the way in which organizational integration and fragmentation are simultaneously taking place. Furthermore, attention is drawn to the methodological difficulty in isolating and measuring components of good quality care. For example, outcome targets concerning the stability or longevity of a placement are limited, as a child's placement with his/her birth parents may be stable, but the child may be subjected to neglect and abuse. Crucially for Smith, in its attempts to provide for vulnerable children and young people, the government fails to give appropriate significance to the less quantifiable or measurable aspects of care. Despite its energetic policy developments, it is Smith's conclusion that the government is failing to keep in focus the qualities that are essential, not only to the positive development of children and young people, but to humanity in general - warmth, empathy, sensitivity and the ability to form trusting relationships. For Smith, the government's approach to future service provision emphasises the modernization of structures, procedures and processes, at the expense of engaging with the messy, moral dilemmas of 'care'.

Note

1. The Fostering Network, the UK's leading charity for everyone involved in fostering, has a membership of almost 50,000 foster carers, local authorities and trusts, independent fostering providers as well as local foster care association.

References

Department for Education and Skills (DfES) (2006) *Care Matters: Transforming the lives of children and young people in care.* London: DfES

Department for Education and Skills (DfES) (2007) *Care Matters: Time for Change.* London: DfES

Dixon, J., Wade, J., Byford, S., Weatherly, H., and Lee, J. (2006) *Young People Leaving Care: A study of costs and outcomes. Report to the Department for Education and Skills.* York: University of York

Farmer, E. and Moyers, S. (forthcoming) *Kinship Care: Fostering effective family and friends placements.* London: Jessica Kingsley

Farmer, E., Moyers, S. and Lipscombe, J. (2004) *Fostering Adolescents.* London: Jessica Kingsley

Fawcett, B., Featherstone, B. and Goddard, J. (2004) *Contemporary Child Care: policy and practice.* Basingstoke: Macmillan

Giddens, A. (1998) *The Third Way: the renewal of social democracy.* Cambridge: Polity Press

Kirton, D. (2007) Step forward? Step back? The professionalization of fostering. *Social Work and Social Sciences Review,* 13, 1, 6-24

Stein, M. (2006) 'Wrong turn', *The Guardian,* 6th December

2

Foster care in transition: From waiting in the wings to centre stage

Carole Smith

Introduction: From Poor Law relief to a professional fostering service

The foundations of foster care in the United Kingdom (UK) lie in the apprenticeships that were established by means of the Poor Law of 1536 and the practice of wet nursing that emerged during the early part of the 19th century (Triseliotis *et al.*, 1995). These largely unregulated and informal arrangements grew into a more formal system of boarding children out with families during the later part of the 19th century. The system was characterised by some degree of selection, supervision and the payment of allowances and continued with much the same purpose and in a similar form until the end of the Second World War. The purpose of boarding out during these years was largely directed to providing homes for destitute children whose parents were dead or missing. Placements were thus intended to be long-term or effectively became so. Today's policies and practices concerning assessment, planning, the facilitation of 'secure attachments' between children and their carers, 'outcomes' for children looked after by the State, and the empowerment of children and their families, are the result of thinking that has developed during the latter half of the twentieth century.

It was arguably the Children Act 1948 that consolidated fostering as a system of support for children and families in need. The Act also emphasised the beneficial effects of fostering as opposed to residential care, and placement in families became the preferred option for children who were looked after by the State. Although foster carers would still be known as foster *parents* for many years to come, their role was changing. A service for families who were recognised as being in some form of physical, emotional or social distress rather than as being simply feckless, required foster carers to co-operate with birth families and social workers in order to achieve formalised goals. This in turn encouraged foster carers to think of themselves as engaged in a form of work where they contributed to gathering information, reviewing progress, considering outcomes and implementing plans – a rather more challenging and publicly visible role than simply acting as everyday parents.

Changes in practice:
From long-term care to diverse provision

It took some years for foster carers' and social workers' practice to evolve. Prosser's (1978) review of research during the previous ten years showed that a majority of foster carers tended to view themselves as substitute parents rather than as providing a service to children and their families. Holman's (1975) well-known research identified the widespread endorsement of an exclusive model of fostering by social workers and foster carers. This approach allowed, if not encouraged, foster carers to assume a parenting role and by virtue of this exclusive relationship to deny the child's status, their relationship with birth families and the desirability of working towards the child's return home. It is unsurprising that foster carers should have adopted this perspective since they operated in a context where social workers often failed to be proactive in planning, decision making and working with parents.

Rowe and Lambert's (1973) early study of 2,812 children in the care of 33 voluntary and statutory agencies in the UK is as noteworthy for its findings about child care planning as it is for its observations about children who were waiting for family placement. The sample comprised children who had been 'in care' for at least six months. Of these children, rehabilitation was anticipated for only around 25% and 61% of children were expected to remain in care until they reached their eighteenth birthday. The DHSS (1985) dissemination of research on practice in 1979-82 conveyed a depressing message about professional planning and decision making. The publication refers to a 'prevailing picture of drift, passivity and lack of planning' (DHSS 1985, 18:5) by social workers who frequently adopted a 'wait and see' approach to making decisions about children admitted to care. Overall, research indicated that fostering placements 'too often' drifted from short to long-term, and there was little proactive work with birth parents. Children in long-term care frequently lost contact with their birth families and had little information or understanding about their pre-care histories and family backgrounds. Similar themes emerged from Prosser's (1978) review of research, which had been completed between 1967 and 1977.

Concern about children drifting in care and waiting for permanent substitute families prepared the ground for UK social workers to import ideas about permanency planning from the USA. There, social workers were initiating decisive permanency planning, which incorporated working agreements with parents, time-limited goals and intensive support to effect rehabilitation. However, a lack of progress towards a child's return home resulted in early decisions about alternative plans in which adoption came to play a significant role. What was known as the 'permanency movement' took off in the UK in the late 1970s and extended into the early 1980s (McKay 1980; Hussell and Monaghan 1982; Morris 1984). Additionally, practitioners in the USA were demonstrating that it was possible to recruit families for children previously considered difficult or impossible to place.

Permanency planning and the enthusiastic recruitment of families for 'hard to place' children is now largely remembered as a drive to increase adoption. However, it also encouraged a sharper focus on the role of foster care as distinct from substitute *parenting* and on the family placement of more challenging children and young people. As early as 1978, Cooper was referring to special projects that were developing to provide family placements for older children with difficult and challenging behaviour, children with disabilities or children who needed a particular type of intervention such as assessment. However, she disputes a sharp distinction between traditional and 'special' fostering practice, suggesting that foster carers had always been sufficiently flexible to take a range of children with varying needs and family circumstances. She remarks that at this time:

Taking the picture as a whole, fostering is now so diversified and dynamic that it is questionable whether 'traditional', 'special' or 'professional' should be regarded as other than developments towards a clearer definition of tasks' (Cooper, 1978, p.51).

Moving into the 1980s, Rowe (1983) chronicled the increasing diversification of fostering tasks and the growing awareness that skill rather than good intentions alone were required to meet the needs of children and young people in care. The recognition that foster carers required appropriate skills and knowledge was accompanied by a greater emphasis on preparation and training. Prosser (1978, pp.33-34) remarks that during the period of her research review, training for foster carers was 'a comparatively recent idea' and was reserved for 'special' fostering programmes. By 1983 Rowe observed that while the provision of training was still concentrated on 'professional' foster carers, in some areas it was provided for all new applicants. However, while commentators on the fostering scene emphasised the importance of adequate training, preparation and support, a review of research conducted since the mid-1970s (Berridge, 1997) still reported 'patchy' provision. Research during this period suggested that many social workers and local authorities still did not see the need for a skilled and 'professional' foster care service. However, reflecting a change in thinking, research conducted between 1997 and 2002 (Sellick and Howell, 2003, p.13) shows that 'the training of foster carers has become an embedded and integral part of the overall service'.

Challenges for foster care and the care system

Thus far, as has been frequently noted, foster care had been viewed as relatively low in status, relying on 'natural' caring abilities, voluntary and altruistic in nature and, apart from 'special' schemes, attracting financial help only to cover the costs of caring for children. In 1997 Sir William Utting referred to the 'isolation and private nature' of foster care as requiring attention in the area of safeguarding children from harm. The early lack of in-depth research has also been attributed to the invisible, private and low status of foster care (Prosser, 1978; Berridge, 1997; National Foster Care Association, 1997a).

This scenario began to change when new research indicated that young people leaving care were significantly disadvantaged. This was particularly so in terms of their social and emotional development, educational performance and post-care ability to function as economically active and self-sustaining citizens (Stein and Carey, 1986; Berridge and Cleaver, 1987; Bonnerjea, 1990; Garnett, 1992; Biehal *et al*, 1992; Heath *et al*, 1994). In 1995 a joint report by the Social Services Inspectorate and the Office for Standards in Education noted:

> The care and education systems in general are failing to promote the educational achievements of children who are looked after. The standards which children achieve are too low and the modest progress they make in primary schools is lost as they proceed through the system. Despite the clear identification of this problem in several research studies and by committees of inquiry, little has been done in practice to boost achievement (quoted in National Foster Care Association, 1997a, p.21).

Although it was recognised that children entering care from disadvantaged, chaotic and dysfunctional families brought many problems with them, it was evident that the care system was ineffective in ameliorating the impact of children's pre-care experience (Department of Health, 1991). Foster carers were clearly implicated in this state of affairs: that is, they were part of a system that involved placement instability (Rowe *et al*, 1984; Stein and Carey, 1986; Garnett, 1990) and poor outcomes for many children. This was particularly apparent as the majority of looked after children were placed with foster carers (from 32% in 1978 to about 65% in the mid-1970s).

Additionally, the care population was on average older than had previously been the case, and many of these young people exhibited challenging and difficult behaviour.

Under these conditions foster care became a matter of public concern. Social Services Inspectorate reports (1995 and 1996), a report from the then National Foster Care Association (NFCA) (1997b) and an investigation by the Association of Directors of Social Services (1997) all pointed to serious problems in delivering an adequate foster care service (1). Overall, the publications identified a shortage of foster carers, such that choice and appropriate matching were difficult to achieve for many children. In particular, the placement needs of older children, sibling groups and black children were particularly hard to meet and this necessarily impacted upon quality of care and placement stability. Problems were identified in the recruitment and retention of foster carers, the level of social work support offered, and the appropriate involvement of foster carers in children's reviews and other planning forums. The National Foster Care Association (1997a) took up the cause, asserting that foster care was in crisis. It argued that in order to remedy this situation, Government should invest in foster care by ensuring the development of a skilled, well supported, properly remunerated and professional workforce. The NFCA (1997a, p.9) said 'a more professional approach is required throughout the foster care service, with foster carers recruited, trained and rewarded on the basis of their skills and experience'. Foster carers should be treated as co-working colleagues by social workers, local authorities and independent agencies.

The most recent research review (Sinclair, 2005) of sixteen studies published or completed since 1998 focused almost exclusively on children who had been looked after by local authorities for at least six months. Some of these studies investigated issues that had been of interest to previous researchers and they found persistent problems reoccurring in foster care provision and the care system. Placement instability continued to cause concern. It was acknowledged that foster care is capable of providing stable long-term placements, which facilitate continuing contact between children and their birth families. However, research conducted during this period indicates that too many children experienced placement disruption and multiple moves (Quinton *et al*, 1998; Thoburn *et al*, 2000; Rushton *et al*, 2001; Farmer *et al*, 2004; Sinclair *et al*, 2004). While placement disruption caused a significant proportion of moves, others resulted from organisational, legal and planning factors in the care system. Choice of placements continued to be problematic in respect of what Sinclair (2005, p.59) terms 'ordinary fostering', that is emergency and short-term placements and some long-term placements that were not considered and confirmed by a placement panel. Research indicates that a choice between placements of this type was only available for around 30% of children needing foster care (Farmer et al, 2004; Sinclair *et al*, 2004).

Educational opportunities and achievement for looked after children also remained problematic. Research in this review identified difficulties associated with attendance, school exclusion and difficult behaviour in school. Children's education was interrupted by placement changes (Cleaver, 2000; Farmer *et al*, 2004; Sinclair *et al* 2004) and foster carers and social workers did not always support and encourage children's achievement at school (Farmer *et al*, 2004; Sinclair *et al* 2004). Some of the studies reflected concerns expressed by the NFCA (1997b) and Sinclair (2005) summarises the issues that influenced foster carers' satisfaction, retention and ability to provide a good quality of care. While some issues related to the nature of fostering itself, many concerned organisational arrangements and cultural attitudes:

> These include considerable dissatisfaction with the fairness, level and nature of pay and allowances; organisational efficiency; and a widespread feeling that carers are neither adequately valued nor treated as members of a team (Sinclair, 2005, p.105).

Challenges and policy responses

The Government has been proactive in responding to many of the problems associated with the care system, including foster care, which have been identified by researchers and other investigators. It introduced the *Quality Protects* programme in England in 1998 and its Welsh counterpart *Children First* was implemented in 1999. The Government's objectives for children's services are a key element of *Quality Protects*. They include high level objectives relating to stable, secure, safe and effective care for all children; good education, health care and social care for looked after children; and the facilitation of young people leaving care to live successful adult lives (see also Secretary of State for Health, 1998). The *Framework for the Assessment of Children in Need and their Families* (Department of Health, Department for Education and Employment and the Home Office, 2000) was introduced with the aims of encouraging evidence-based practice and sharpening social workers analytical and decision-making skills. It seeks to ensure that assessment is focused on children's developmental needs, on their parents' capacity to meet these needs and on family and environmental factors that impact on children's wellbeing. The Children (Leaving Care) Act 2000 was implemented in 2002 with a range of measures to prepare and support care leavers and the Care Standards Act 2000 provides for monitoring and inspection of all social services and independent social care provision. Additionally, the Adoption and Children Act 2002, implemented in full in December 2005, updates the 1976 adoption legislation and informs the Government's drive to increase the number of children adopted from care.

National Minimum Standards have been introduced for foster care and the *Choice Protects* grant to local authorities between 2003 and 2006 was designed to 'strengthen their overall fostering services and to improve the quality and choice of placements for looked after children' (Department for Education and Skills, 2006). As further recognition of foster carers' significant contribution (and expressed dissatisfaction) the Government published national minimum financial allowances, with an implementation date of April 2007, to cover the real cost of fostering a child or young person. *Every Child Matters* (Chief Secretary to the Treasury, 2003) and the Children Act 2004 have introduced numerous organisational, workforce development and practice imperatives that are designed to help all children achieve the five outcomes relating to being healthy, staying safe, enjoying and achieving, making a positive contribution and economic wellbeing. The Government has developed the common assessment framework and the integrated children's system with the intention of supporting multidisciplinary assessment and intervention. Professional decision-making and planning should stay sharply focused on helping children achieve the five outcomes in *Every Child Matters*.

The clarity of Government's priorities for service development, assessment, planning and intervention for looked after children is further underpinned by National Priorities Guidance and Public Service Agreements. Early national objectives for children's social services were identified in *Modernising Social Services* (Secretary of State for Health, 1998). In 1999 the Government introduced a National Priorities Guidance target to reduce, by 2001, the number of looked after children who had three or more placement moves in a year to no more than sixteen per cent. In 2004 it added a new Public Service Agreement target aimed at improving placement stability and educational achievement for children looked after for over two and a half years. This is intended to:

Narrow the gap in educational achievement between looked after children and that of their peers, and improve their educational support and the stability of their lives so that by 2008, 80% of children under 16 who have been looked after for 2.5 or more years will have been living in the same placement for at least two years, or are placed for adoption (Department for Children, Schools and Families, 2007, p.4).

Conclusion: Foster care (finally) at centre stage

As has been noted above, foster care started as a relatively invisible and informal activity and there have been many complaints over time that it has remained invisible to policy makers and researchers. Lobbyists, such as the NFCA (1997a), focused attention on the urgent need to recognise and respond to problems in the foster care service. *Every Child Matters* (Chief Secretary to the Treasury, 2003) emphasises the importance of recruitment, training, support and paid leave for foster carers to enable the provision of high quality, stable placements and choice in placement provision. However, the Green Paper, *Care Matters* (Secretary of State for Education and Skills, 2006) shifts the role of foster care to centre stage as part of its recommendations for improving the performance of the care system as a whole. The subsequent White Paper, *Care Matters: Time for Change* (Secretary of State for Education and Skills 2007) continues the focus on foster care and placement stability as being central to achieving valued outcomes for looked after children.

Despite the long history of research on outcomes for looked after children, and a plethora of policy initiatives, *Care Matters* still reports that too many children and young people experience placement instability and poor educational, social and economic outcomes. It refers to 'the shocking statistics on the education of children in care' (p. 5, p.1) and the 'bleak' life chances of children who have been looked after (p. 13, p.1.13). In summary:

The long-term outcomes of children in care are also devastating. They are over represented in a range of vulnerable groups including those not in education, employment or training post-16, teenage parents, young offenders, drug users and prisoners (Secretary of State for Education and Skills, 2006: 5: 2).

Foster carers now look after over 70% of children and young people in the care system (Department for Children, Schools and Families 2007). There is also a demonstrable relationship between stable placements, children's experience of security and permanence and their educational achievement and social wellbeing. It is not surprising therefore, that foster care must play a significant role in helping to improve the life chances of looked after children and young people. With this in mind, *Care Matters* suggests measures to improve the quality and organisation of the foster care service. It identifies the development of a tiered model of foster care provision where carers would be trained and skilled to different degrees, enabling them to be matched with the level of challenge and complexity presented by individual children. This would be underpinned by a new system of competency-based skills and qualifications incorporating the principles of social pedagogy, revised National Minimum Standards, a new fees structure to reflect the demands of operating in each tier and a mandatory national registration scheme for foster carers. In order to improve placement choice and availability, the Government explores ways of enhancing the recruitment of foster carers, establishing regional commissioning units and making more extensive use of placements with family and friends. The NFCA (1997a, p.36) recommended a tiered model of foster care 'through which carers could progress, developing skills and being appropriately paid at each level' in its drive, ten years ago, to professionalise the service. Now, it would seem that foster carers may be promised a career with corresponding entitlements to skills training, appropriate payment, organisational and professional support, leave arrangements and career progression. Mandatory registration would put them 'on a par with their colleagues in social work, residential care and other parts of the children's workforce' (Secretary of State for Education and Skills, 2006, p.49). Although the White Paper (Secretary of State for Education and Skills 2007) emphasises many of these themes, it fails to incorporate them all. However, it retains a particular emphasis on training, support and skills development for foster carers. In short, foster care in the UK today has now achieved public recognition of its central role in making the care system work for the wellbeing of looked after children. How far this recognition translates into a *professional* foster care service in the sense that the National Foster Care Association demanded in 1997, remains to be seen.

Note

1. The National Foster Care Association is now known as the Fostering Network.

References

Association of Directors of Social Services (1997) *The Foster Care Market: A National Perspective*, Ipswich: ADSS.

Berridge, D. (1997) *Foster Care: A Research Review*, London: The Stationery Office.

Berridge, D. and Cleaver, H. (1987) *Foster Home Breakdown*, Oxford: Blackwell.

Biehal, N., Clayden, J., Stein, M. and Wade, J. (1992) *Prepared for Living? A Survey of Young People Leaving the Care of Three Local Authorities*, London: National Children's Bureau.

Bonnerjea, L. (1990) *Leaving Care in London*, London Boroughs Children's Regional Planning Committee.

Chief Secretary to the Treasury (2003) *Every Child Matters*, London: The Stationery Office.

Cleaver, H. (2000) *Fostering Family Contact: A Study of Children, Parents and Foster Carers*, London: The Stationery Office.

Cooper, J. (1978) *Patterns of Family Placement: Current Issues in Fostering and Adoption*, London:National Children's Bureau.

Department for Education and Skills (2006) The Children Act 1989 Report 2004 and 2005, London: DFES.

Department for Children, Schools and Families (2007) National Statistics: Children Looked after in England: Year Ending 31 March 2007, London: DCSF.

Department of Health (1991) *Patterns and Outcomes in Child Placement: Messages from Current research and their Implications*, London: HMSO.

Department of Health and Social Security (1985) *Social Work Decisions in Child Care: Recent Research Findings and their Implications*, London: HMSO.

Department of Health, Department for Education and Employment and the Home Office (2000) Framework for the Assessment of Children in Need and their Families, London: The Stationery Office.

Farmer, E., Moyers, S. and Lipscombe, J. (2004) *Fostering Adolescents*, London: Jessica Kingsley Publishers.

Garnett, L. (1990) *Leaving Care for Independence: A Follow-up Study to the Placement Outcomes Project*, Report to the Department of Health.

Garnett, L. (1992) *Leaving Care and After*, London: National Children's Bureau.

Heath, A., Colton, M. and Aldgate, J. (1994) 'The educational progress of children in and out of care' *British Journal of Social Work*, 19(6) 447-460.

Holman, B. (1975) 'The place of fostering in social work', *British Journal of Social Work*, 5(1), 4-29.

Hussell, C. and Monaghan, B. (1982) 'Going for Good', *Social Work To-day* 13(47) 7-9.

McKay, M. (1980) 'Planning for permanent placement', *Adoption and Fostering*, 99: 19-21.

Morris, C. (1984) *The Permanency Principle in Child Care Social Work*, Norwich: University of East Anglia.

National Foster Care Association (1997a) *Foster Care in Crisis*, London: NFCA.

National Foster Care Association (1997b) *The Organisation of Fostering Services*, London: NFCA.

Prosser, H. (1978) *Perspectives on Foster Care*, Windsor: NFER Publishing Company.

Quinton, D., Rushton, A., Dance, C. and Mayes, D. (1998) *Joining New Families: A Study of Adoption and Fostering in Middle Childhood*, Chichester: John Wiley.

Rowe, J. (1983) *Fostering in the Eighties*, London: British Agencies for Adoption and Fostering.

Rowe, J. and Lambert, L. (1973) *Children who Wait*, London: Association of British Adoption Agencies.

Rowe, J., Cain, H., Hundleby, M. and Keane, A. (1984) *Long Term Foster Care*, Batsford/British Agencies for Adoption and Fostering.

Rushton, A., Dance, C., Quinton, D. and Mayes, D. (2001) *Siblings in Late Permanent Placements*, London; British Agencies for Adoption and Fostering.

Secretary of State for Education and Skills (2006) *Care Matters: Transforming the*

Lives of Children and Young People in Care, London: The Stationery Office.

Secretary of State for Education and Skills (2007) Care Matters: Time for Change, London: The Stationery Office.

Secretary of State for Health (1998) *Modernising Social Services*, London: The Stationery Office.

Sellick, C. and Howell, D. (2003) *Innovative, Tried and Tested: A Review of Good Practice in Fostering*, London: Social Care Institute for Excellence.

Sinclair, I., Gibbs, I. and Wilson, K. (2004) *Foster Placements: Why they Succeed and Why they Fail*, London: Jessica Kingsley Publications.

Sinclair, I. (2005) *Fostering Now: Messages from Research*, London: Jessica Kingsley Publications.

Social Services Inspectorate (1996) *Inspection of Local Authority Fostering 1995-96 National Summary Report*, London: Department or Health.

Social Services Inspectorate and Office for Standards in Education (1995) *The Education of Children who are Looked after by Local Authorities*, London: SSI/OFSTED.

Stein, M. and Carey, K. (1986) Leaving Care, Oxford: Blackwell

Thoburn, J., Norford, L., and Parvez Rashid, S. (2000) *Permanent Family Placement for Children of Minority Ethnic Origin*, London: Jessica Kingsley Publishers.

Triseliotis, J., Sellick, C. and Short, R. (1995) *Foster Care: Theory and Practice*, London: Batsford/British Agencies for Adoption and Fostering.

Utting, Sir William (1997) *People Like Us*, London: The Stationery Office.

3
Children of the State:
Reforming the care system. New Labour and corporate parenting

Elizabeth Harlow and Nick Frost

Introduction

Since coming to power in 1997, the New Labour government of the United Kingdom (UK) has pursued a reform agenda informed by an ideological approach known as 'the third way'. Aiming to offer a middle path between the politically left and right (Giddens, 2006), the third way: demands a balance between rights and responsibilities; promotes independence through work; provides for genuine need; and encourages lifelong learning. This approach is associated with the construction of the 'social investment state' (Giddens, 1998, cited in Fawcett et al., 2004). That is, the population is understood as human capital, and state investment should facilitate social inclusion, particularly by means of participation in the employment market, as opposed to welfare dependency and social exclusion. In order to encourage independence and active participation in employment, the state is investing in a healthy and educated workforce (Jordan with Jordan, 2000, drawing on the work of Carling, 1999). This ideological foundation has informed the modernisation of the welfare services in general and the services to children and their families in particular (Anning et al,, 2006).

The goal that all children should reach their potential and become fully included and participating members of society is enshrined in the *Every Child Matters* policy (DfES, 2004) and related Children Act, 2004. This overarching policy framework and legislation requires local agencies to co-operate with a view to: improving the physical and mental health and emotional well-being of children; protecting children from harm and neglect; providing them with education, training and recreation; facilitating their contribution to society; and facilitating their social and economic well-being. Whilst it is expected that universal services will meet the needs of most children, children with more complex needs, such as those who are looked after by the local authority, will be offered focussed assistance.

The focussed assistance required by looked after children was set out in the Green Paper *Care Matters: Transforming the lives of children and young people in care* which was published in 2006 (DfES, 2006a). The issues that informed the content of this Green Paper as well as the proposed policy directions were discussed at a symposium held in March 2007 at the University of Salford. A version of this paper was presented by Nick Frost, Professor of Social Work (Children, childhood and families) at Leeds Metropolitan University, as a 'scene setting' introduction to the discussion. Here attention will be drawn to the ways in which the state has failed to act as a 'good parent' and research findings that have shown that young people cared for by the state have been at a heightened risk of becoming socially excluded as adults. The content of the Green Paper and subsequent White Paper *Care Matters: A time of change* (DfES, 2007) which aims to resolve this situation will then be outlined. Before the paper is concluded, some of the criticisms of the government's proposals will be acknowledged. Inevitably a relatively brief article limits the content of the discussion and only a few of the policy initiatives can be addressed here: these are, child care placements, social work services, and the education of looked after children.

The state as parent

Throughout history there have always been occasions when a particular child could not be cared for by his/her own parents. On such occasions parental care has been assumed or shared, formally or informally, by kith and kin, charities, or the state. At this point in the discussion, the focus is not on why the state might take on the role of parent, but on how it carries out the responsibilities it has assumed. In the past, it was considered acceptable for the state to provide care by means of institutions. Since the 1950s, however, theoretical developments, empirical research findings and scandals have thrown this option into disfavour. Attachment theory (Bowlby, 1951) challenged the appropriateness of institutional settings, particularly for young children, on the grounds that they did not facilitate the development of a close relationship, an essential requirement for sound psychological development. In consequence, the placing of children with substitute or foster families has become the preferred form of state provision. Whilst Utting (1991) concluded that there remained a need for some residential care, as some children could not or should not be placed with families, scandals (for example, Levy and Kahan, 1991; Kirkwood, 1993) have not encouraged its use. Despite government initiatives and academic contributions encouraging the improvement of practice in residential settings and the appreciation of its contribution (see for example, Utting, 1997; Whittaker et al., 1998; The Violence Against Children Study Group, 1999; Berridge, 2002) it has continued to be an option of last resort (Jackson, 2002).

Although substitute family care may be considered a more attractive alternative to residential care, research has shown that the rate of disruption in foster placements could be as high as 50% (Trasler, 1960; Parker, 1966; George, 1970; Napier, 1972, all cited in Simmonds, 1988). More recent research findings continue to show a high level of disruption (Selwyn and Quinton, 2004). The general level of placement disruption, irrespective of setting, has increased over recent times. Since the introduction of the Children Act 1989, the rate of placement change has doubled (Packman and Hall, 1998 cited in Jackson, 2002). Biehal et al. (1995) found that only one in ten of the young people in her research sample had remained in the same placement throughout their care career whilst '10 per cent had moved more than ten times' (Biehal et al., 1995, cited in Jackson, 2002, p.39). Between 1995 and 2000, the average number of placements experienced by those in the care system increased from 2.9 to 3.5 (DH, 2001, cited in Jackson, 2002). It has recently been concluded that some children who are looked after by the state experience as many as three placements in one year (DfES 2006b, cited in Munro & Hardy, 2007).

Placement change can occur for a variety of reasons. Drawing on the available research, Jackson (2002) suggests that a placement may breakdown if a child or young person requests a move or more usually if the residential workers or foster carers refuse to continue providing accommodation. This latter example may be associated with the behaviour of the young person. Very often, however, moves are dictated by local policies, for instance, they may be the result of rules concerning short-term and long-term foster care or the closure of residential establishments. In terms of the latter, financial imperatives may be at work. In addition, the local authority does not always have control over the length of a placement, and delays in court procedures can impact negatively by preventing the move to a permanent arrangement. The rate of placement change has become an issue because numerous moves are considered to be detrimental to a child's development. Citing the work of Parker et al. (1991) and Harwin and Owen (2003), Selwyn and Quinton (2004, p.7) confirm the view that placement 'stability has been linked to better outcomes for children'. In consequence, the Department for Education and Skills recently commissioned a review of the literature on patterns of placement stability (see Munro & Hardy, 2007). With reference to the work of Bowlby (see above), numerous placement moves are seen as inhibiting a child's ability to development and maintain relationships. Frequent change may make it difficult for a child to achieve a positive individual and social identity as contact with his/her family and community, as well as knowledge of his/her past may have been lost (see for example, Rowe et al., 1984, cited in Simmonds, 1988). Rapid turnover of social workers may also be detrimental. Furthermore, consistency in education and health care is considered beneficial if a child is to reach his or her potential. Although the state may have attempted to act as a good parent, research has shown that for many children stability and continuity of care has not been guaranteed. In addition, the state has also been criticised for expecting young people to become independent prematurely and for failing to support them adequately as they make the transition to adulthood (Wade, 2003). This may compound and/or contribute to the difficulties experienced by young people as they leave care to live independently.

The following summary of key research findings highlights the difficulties for specific categories of care leavers:

- Many care leavers have lower educational attainment, higher unemployment rates, more unstable career patterns and greater dependency on welfare benefits than other young people.
- Young women leaving care aged between 16 and 19 are more likely to be young mothers than other young women of that age group.
- Black, Asian and mixed-heritage young people may face additional problems due to lack of contact with their families and communities as well as experiencing racism.
- Young disabled people leaving care may experience abrupt or delayed transitions from care due to restricted housing and employment options and inadequate support (Stein, 2002, p.61).

In consequence, young care leavers are at a heightened risk of becoming socially excluded adults.

Improving state parenthood

It is important to acknowledge that since coming into office in 1997 the New Labour government has consistently been attempting to improve the quality of the care it has offered. The Quality Protects (QP) Programme (DH, 1998), was in part a response to scandals concerning abuse in residential care settings. Between 1999 and 2004 an investment of £885 million was made in the child care system on the basis of each local authority's detailed annual 'management action plans'. A core feature of QP was improving outcomes for looked after children that were measured by performance indicators. There was a particular focus on educational achievement and support for care leavers. Further support was offered to young people by means of the Children (Leaving Care) Act passed in 2000. It is by means of the Care Matters policy initiative, however, that the government has explicitly committed the state to improving outcomes for looked after children by providing the highest standards of corporate parenting:

> The State has a unique responsibility for children in care. It has taken on the task of parenting some of society's most vulnerable children and in doing so it must become everything a good parent should be (DfES, 2006a, 1.1)

> A good corporate parent must offer everything that a good parent would provide and more, addressing both the difficulties which the children experience and the challenges of parenting within a complex system of services (DfES, 2007, 1.20)

As indicated above, the *Care Matters* initiative aims to improve the state's performance as corporate parent by means of varied measures. The measures summarised here appertain to the enhancement of continuity in the lives of looked after children as well as the aim to increase the educational achievement of care leavers (see DfES, 2007).

The White Paper gives importance to the role of social worker in the state's performance as parent. Social workers are central to the provision of continuity. For children placed away form home they provide a crucial facilitative link with their families and communities. They can also act as an important, relational 'bridge' if placement change has to occur. In consequence, it is proposed that social workers should visit the children in their care more often, irrespective of placement type. Given that at present social workers have only limited time for direct contact, the White Paper proposes that the Children's Workforce Development Council and the General Social Care Council should collaborate in the remodelling of the social care workforce. Finally, the establishment of new organisational partnerships termed 'social work practices' should be piloted on the basis that these independent arrangements might improve the delivery of social work services.

Given that a child is most likely to experience stability in the home of his/her birth parents (Schofield et al., 2000) the government proposes to invest resources in returning a child home whenever possible. In order to help children and young people to retain relationships with their own family and members of their community, it is proposed that local authorities should not be allowed to place them outside of their own locality unless it is in their best interests to do so. Furthermore, perhaps reflecting the recommendations that the local authority should use a wide range of placements, including residential (Laming, undated), specialist commissioning units should be established. It is intended that a greater number and variety of placements in each locality, will reduce the need to place children at a geographical distance. Finally, continuity in education is emphasised and it is proposed that a local authority's care planning should not disrupt a child's education. Moves between schools in years ten and eleven when crucial work for examinations is being undertaken should only occur in exceptional circumstances.

In addition to facilitating continuity in education as identified above, proposals within the White Paper aiming to improve the educational outcomes of young people include:

- High quality early years education should be available for all children in care
- A review of the educational position of children in care should take place in the academic year 2008-9
  Children in care should only be excluded from school as a last resort
- Alternative provision for excluded children in care should be available from the first day of exclusion
- The National Minimum Standards for foster and residential care relating to education should be raised
- The role of the designated teacher for children in care should be strengthened
- There should be a virtual school head teacher for children in care in each local authority
- Personal Education Plans should be established for all children in care
- Funding to pay for extra help for children in care who are not reaching their targets should be made available
- Specified services should be extended for children in care
- Home-school agreements should be enhanced
- There should be an improvement in services for children in care who are deemed to have 'special educational needs' (DfES, 2007, 4.10-4.56)

This brief summary hardly does justice to the width and depth of the *Care Matters* proposals relating to the education of children in care. In addition to what has been described, there are a range of proposals relating to further and higher education. In total, this appears to be a fundamental attempt on the part of the government to address poor educational outcomes for the care population. Despite this, critical comments on the White Paper have been made and it is to these analyses that attention is now turned.

Care Matters: Critical perspectives

Whilst the *Care Matters* initiative has in general been welcomed by lobby groups and voluntary organizations, two critiques have emerged. These critiques concern firstly, the plans for the making of social work independent of local authorities and secondly the reliance on 'outcome' evaluation.

As indicated above, it has been proposed that Directors of Children's Service should commission or purchase social work services from small, independent practices of social workers. The proposed arrangement of these practices appears to be similar to that of General Practitioners in the National Health Service (NHS). According to the *Green Paper*, social workers operating independently from the local authority might provide a more flexible and therefore improved service (DfES, 2006a, 3.17). However, the problems in social work provision concern the lack of continuity in the relationship between practitioners and children (Le Grand, 2006). Social workers do not see children enough and they do not see the same social worker over a period of time. This latter problem results from too high a turnover of staff: dissatisfaction with the deterioration in their employment context means that social workers are leaving their posts (see Harlow, 2004). This problem may be the consequence of excessive bureaucracy and the dominance of managerialism. This might stem from either poor management at the local level, which could be resolved within the current organisational form, or from the demands of central government, which would also impact upon independent practices. In short, re-organisation and the creation of independent practices may either not be necessary or may not provide the solution (Le Grand, 2006). Social workers as representatives of the corporate parent do not have to work in independent organisations in order to provide a good service.

Toynbee (2006) is also critical of this proposal on three main grounds. Firstly, there is enough reform in children's services taking place in the UK at the moment. The *Every Child Matters* agenda is demanding, but progress is being made and this progress should not be disrupted. Secondly, the proposed reforms would create extra costs. In addition to the cost of the social work services, there would be the cost of the commissioning body. Finally, according to Toynbee, similar organisational experiments in the NHS have largely failed. For Toynbee then the system should be left largely as it is with the *Every Child Matters* reforms being given the opportunity to take effect. It might also be argued that the proposal for independent social work services would create fragmentation and erect barriers between the practices and the rest of the local authority provision. This would occur at a time when the more general shift is towards 'joining-up' services (see Frost, 2005).

The second critique concerns the over-reliance on the simplistic measurement of outcomes for care leavers that underpin the *Care Matters* proposals (Stein, 2006). Although Stein has advocated for improvements in corporate parenting, particularly in relation to young people leaving care (Stein, 1997; Stein & Wade, 2000), he is critical of the state care being held solely responsible for their long term welfare. According to Stein (2006), holding state care as solely responsible is flawed because firstly, many young people only spend a brief period in care and this brief period cannot be expected to have any significant impact on their long term welfare or educational achievement. Secondly, many of those who leave care between the ages of sixteen and eighteen come into care between the ages of ten and fifteen years, often from disadvantaged backgrounds and with already disrupted educations. Thirdly, there needs to be a distinction between three groups of care leavers: those who move on – and often have successful outcomes; those who 'survive' and may do well if adequately supported; and those who are highly vulnerable – who form perhaps five per cent of the care population, but whom are strongly associated with a 'failing' care system (see Action for Aftercare, 2004). Fourthly, outcomes may improve as young people mature. Having surmounted the usual challenges of youth, some care leavers may achieve personal objectives and become fully participating members of society. In consequence, longitudinal research is required in order that outcomes for care leavers might be more fully explored. Finally, current outcomes measures are too crude as they detach young people from their backgrounds and fail to take into account the difficulties they have already endured.

Both Toynbee (2006) and Stein (2006) conclude that the children and young people who are cared for by the state have to be understood in the light of their background. This means that any assessment of the state as corporate parent has to take this into account, but also attempts to improve the social inclusion of care leavers must address the wider social issues such as poverty and a poor education system in general.

Conclusion

The proposals outlined in both the Green and White papers are further indication of the UK government's attempt to reform and modernise the organisation and delivery of welfare services. Without any empirical evidence to support the measure, the shift towards the independence of social work services to 'looked after' children appears to be ideologically driven. Whether this stance is more reflective of neo-liberalism than the 'third way' ideology that is said to inform New Labour is a point for discussion. Nevertheless, the 'third way' as described above, is clearly evident in the *Care Matters* agenda.

In order to reduce the risks of young care experienced people becoming socially excluded, the government is taking seriously its responsibility as a corporate parent and attempting to improve its performance. By attending to the question of placement stability and relational continuity, the state is endeavouring to provide positive foundations from which children and young people can develop. By investing in the education of children in care as well as assessing and purposively managing their progress into post-school provision, it is intended that qualifications and training will facilitate long term employment and non-dependence on the state. In this way, young people with experience of the care system will take on their responsibilities as citizens and become active social participants.

Although there have been criticisms of the government's proposals, there is a good deal to be applauded. In particular, there has been a distinct shift away from the stigmatised, minimalist approach that historically informed the provision that was made available to children who were unable to live with their families. In addition to new policies, plans and material resources, the emphasis on the state as corporate parent is enhanced. The state as parent is represented, not only by central and local government, but all members of the children's workforce. All of these professionals are now explicitly required to, not only 'care for', but 'care about' the state's children (DfES, 2007).

References

Anning, A., Cottrell, D., Green, J., Frost, N., and Robinson, M. (2006) *Developing Multidisciplinary Teamwork for Integrated Children's Services*. London: Open University Press.

Action for Aftercare (2004) *Setting The Agenda: What's left to do in leaving care*. London: National Children's Homes.

Berridge, D. (2002) Residential care. in D. McNeish, T. Newman, and H. Roberts (Eds.) *What Works for Children?* Buckingham: Open University Press.

Biehal, N., Clayden, J., Stein, M., and Wade, J. (1995) *Moving On: Young People and Leaving Care Schemes*. London: HMSO

Bowlby, J. (1951) *Maternal Care and Mental Health*. Geneva: World Health Organization.

Carling, A. (1999) New Labour's polity: Tony Giddens and the 'Third Way'. *Imprints: Journal of Analytical Socialism*, 3, 3, 214-242

Department for Education and Skills (DfES) (2004) *Every Child Matters: Change for children*. London: DfES

Department for Education and Skills (DfES) (2006a) *Care Matters: Transforming the lives of children and young people in care.* London: DfES

Department for Education and Skills (DfES) (2006b) *Statistics of Education: Children Looked After by Local Authorities Year Ending 31 March 2005 Volume 1: National Tables.* London: DfES

Department for Education and Skills (DfES) (2007) *Care Matters: Time for Change.* London: DfES

Department of Health (1998) *Quality Protects.* London: The Stationary Office

Department of Health (DH) (2001) *Children Looked After by Local Authorities Year Ending March 31 2000* London: DH

Fawcett, B., Featherstone, B., and Goddard, J. (2004) *Contemporary Child Care: Policy and practice.* Basingstoke: Palgrave Macmillan

Frost, N. (2005) *Partnership, Professionalism and Joined-up Thinking.* Dartington: Research in Practice

George, V. (1970) *Foster Care Theory and Practice.* London: Routledge and Kegan Paul

Giddens, A. (1998) *The Third Way: The renewal of social democracy.* Cambridge: Polity Press.

Giddens, A. (2006) *Sociology.* (5th ed.) Cambridge: Polity Press

Harlow, E. (2004) Why don't social workers want to be social workers anymore? New managerialism, postfeminism and the shortage of social workers in Social Services Departments in England and Wales, *European Journal of Social Work,* 7, 2, 167-179

Harwin, J. and Owen, M. (2003) The implementation of care plans and its relationship to child welfare. *Child and Family Quarterly,* 1, (1, 71-83

Jackson, S. (2002) Promoting stability and continuity in care away from home. in D. McNeish, T. Newman, and H. Roberts (Eds.) *What Works for Children?* Buckingham: Open University Press

Jordon, B. with Jordon, C. (2000) *Social Work and the Third Way. Tough love as social policy.* London: Sage.

Kirkwood, A. (1993) *The Leicestershire Enquiry.* Leicester: Leicester County Council

Laming, H. (undated) *Care Matters: Placements working group report.* www. dcsf.gov.uk/publications/timeforchange. accessed 2/4/08

Le Grand, J. (undated) *Consistent Care Matters: Exploring the potential of social work practices: Executive summary.* www.dcsf.gov.uk/publications/ timeforchange/ accessed 2/4/08.

Levey, A. and Kahan, B. (1991) *The Pindown Experience and the Protection of Children: Report of the Staffordshire Child Care Inquiry.* Stafford: Staffordshire County Council

Munro, E. and Hardy, A. (2007) *Placement Stability: A Review of the Literature.* Loughborough: Loughborough University, Centre for Child and Family Research.

Napier, H. (1972) Success and failure in foster care. *British Journal of Social Work,* 2, 2

Packman, J, and Hall, C, (1998) *From Care to Accommodation: Support, protection and control in child care.* London: Stationary Office

Parker, R.A. (1966) *Decision in Child Care.* George London: Allen and Unwin

Parker, R., Ward, H. and Jackson, S (1991) (Eds.) *Looking After Children: Assessing outcomes in child care.* London: HMSO

Rowe, J., Cain., Hundleby, M. and Keane, A. (1984) *Long-term Fostering.* London: Batsford/British Agencies for Adoption and Fostering

Selwyn, J. and Quinton, D. (2004) Stability, permanence, outcomes and support: Foster care and adoption compared. *Adoption and Fostering,* 28, 4, 6-15

Schofield, G., Beek, M., and Sargent, K. with Thoburn, J. (2000) *Growing Up in Foster Care.* London: British Agencies for Fostering and Adoption.

Simmonds, J. (1988) Social work with children: Developing a framework for responsible practice. in J. Aldgate and J. Simmonds (Eds.) *Direct Work with Children: A guide for social work practitioners.* London: Batsford

Stein, M. (1997) *What Works in Leaving Care?* Barkingside: Barnardo's

Stein, M. (2002) Leaving care. in D. McNeish, T. Newman and H. Roberts (Eds.) *What Works for Children?* Buckingham: Open University Press

Stein, M. (2006) Wrong turn. *The Guardian,* 6th December

Stein, M. and Wade, J. (2000) Helping care leavers: Problems and strategic responses. London: Department of Health

The Violence Against Children Study Group (1999) *Children, Child Abuse and Child Protection. Placing children centrally.* Chichester: Wiley

Toynbee, P. (2006) We can't let children in care fall victim to privatisation. *The Guardian,* 10th October

Trasler, G. (1960) *In Place of Parents.* London: Routledge and Kegan Paul

Utting, W (1991) *Children in the Public Care: A review of residential child care.* London:HMSO

Utting, W. (1997) *People Like Us. The report of the Review of the Safeguards for Children Living Away from Home.* London: The Stationary Office

Wade, J. (2003) *Leaving Care* Totnes: Research in Practice.

Whittaker, D. Archer, L. and Hicks, L. (1998) *Working in Children's Homes. Challenges and complexities.* Chichester: Wiley

4
Towards a mixed economy of foster care provision

Clive Sellick

Introduction

Foster care in the UK, and especially in England, is no longer a public sector activity supplemented only by voluntary child care organizations. Somewhere in the region of twenty per cent of all looked after children are placed with foster carers attached to a range of non-governmental fostering agencies (DfES, 2005a). Known collectively as independent fostering providers (IFPs), these organisations assess, approve, train and supervise foster carers and provide, for payment, foster placements and therapeutic and educational services to local authorities for children and young people in their care or accommodation (Sellick, 2005, p.2). A national survey of IFPs in 2001 (Sellick and Connolly, 2001, 2002) and a review of fostering practice across the UK for the Social Care Institute for Excellence in 2003 (Sellick and Howell, 2003, 2004) illustrated the significant growth of these agencies in both the traditional voluntary child care sector and the rapidly expanding private sector.

The expansion in the use of IFP placements can be attributed to two main factors. Firstly, as fostering has become the principal placement of choice, most local authorities across the UK have experienced a chronic shortage of foster carers (Waterhouse, 1997; Triseliotis *et al*, 2000; Swain, 2005). Secondly, since the beginning of the New Labour government in 1997, policy has shifted incrementally towards commissioning services for children, including fostering, from outside the public sector (Sellick and Connolly, 2002).

The green light to IFP usage had already been given sometime before the change of government. Social Services Inspectors had reported in 1995, for example, that these agencies 'represent a new and expanding source of foster placements' (Department of Health, 1995, p.14). However, a much stronger steer came from the Secretary of State in 2001 who said that 'For too long, in my view, there has been a stand off in the relationship between the statutory, private and voluntary care sectors. There should be no ideological barriers getting in the way of the best care for vulnerable people' (Department of Health, 2001). Whilst launching the new *Choice Protects* initiative in the following year, the Minister of Health spoke of the importance, of 'helping councils commission and deliver effective placements and the contribution of the independent fostering agencies' (Department of Health, 2002b). Little wonder perhaps that the independent fostering sector expanded rapidly during this period from 62 agencies in 1998 to 265 in 2005 (Sellick, 2006b). The Green Paper (Department for Education and Skills, 2006) has cemented these steps: it includes proposals for piloting new regional commissioning units of services building upon existing arrangements.

The difficulties faced by many local authorities in finding an adequate supply of foster carers led most to purchase IFP placements, often at short notice and in emergencies, on what has been called a 'spot-purchased basis' (Sellick, 1999, Kirton *et al*, 2003, Sellick and Howell, 2004). This method of commissioning has three major deficits. Firstly, it does not allow IFPs to predict likely demand or local authorities to predict cost. Secondly, it effectively prohibits both the local authority commissioners and the independent providers from planning for their respective needs and services. Thirdly, it takes little account of the individual needs of children or the particular strengths of their prospective foster carers. As Petrie and Wilson found in their study of children's day care and fostering services 'the use of spot purchasing as a major distributive mechanism merely reflects the fact that children are slotted in wherever there is a vacancy with little opportunity for matching or choice' (Petrie and Wilson, 1999, p.194).

Another approach for commissioning fostering services is known as 'outsourcing' where public authorities transfer responsibility for all or most of their provision to non governmental agencies. Although largely absent in the United Kingdom (UK), this approach has been tried and tested in parts of the United States of America and Australia (Barber, 2002, Unruh and Hodgkin, 2004). Researchers in both countries found two main problems - it encourages the establishment of a few, large agencies which successfully manipulate and monopolise the market and, related to this, the range and diversity of services are reduced.

A third approach (and in the New Labour lexicon, a 'middle-way') has emerged whereby local authorities and IFPs have entered into contracting or service level arrangements with one another. These arrangements allow them to minimise the risks of both spot purchasing and outsourcing by planning for the purchase and provision of an agreed range, set and number of services. In his study of these emerging agreements, Sellick proposed a commissioning framework which would avoid the combined pitfalls of the other two approaches. He stated:

> The establishment of small networks of local authorities and IFPs was commonly seen as the most effective framework for commissioning from the respondents in this study. Although mostly regional, these networks might include some more distant IFPs where local authorities required long-term or very specialist placements. Such networks of agencies allow local authorities and IFPs to contract with two or three partner agencies. This would go some way to avoiding the risks of monopolies identified in the American and Australian studies. Within each network, commissioned services would be identified and planned and include the full range of fostering placements according to local need (Sellick, 2005, p.12).

The major question, which the rest of this chapter examines, is whether this framework has a chance to succeed or whether other, ever-strengthening, forces driving policy and practice will shape a quite different commissioning model. Previous studies, particularly over the past decade, have charted the factors which underpinned the emergence and establishment of IFPs. This chapter reflects upon these studies, but also considers contemporary pragmatic, ideological, managerial and political forces in order to speculate about the nature and location of future fostering service provision in Britain.

Supplementing or exploiting shortfalls in public provision?

Successive publications have charted the increasing proportion of children and young people who were fostered and the correspondingly decreasing proportion that were placed in residential or other non-family based care (Sellick *et al*, 2004, Wilson *et al*, 2004, Sellick, 2006a). As this practice progressed, flaws in the system began to appear with accounts of placement instability and lack of placement choice for matching children's needs with foster carers' skills. A kind of structural fault seemed to have appeared in which the virtual absence of placement alternatives to foster care had led to a chronic shortage of foster carers across most of the UK. As fostering became the principal placement of choice, and despite foster carer shortages, there was an inevitable steer towards using mainstream foster carers for ever larger numbers of young people with significant emotional difficulties. These young people often demonstrated behaviour that required a range of responsive, therapeutic and educational services in addition to stable foster care placements. The independent fostering agencies were quick to recognize and act upon this and offer the kind of provision identified in an early evaluation of one of the first IFPs (Sellick, 1999, Sellick and Connolly, 1999).

Another aspect of this monopoly practice, and one which allowed the IFPs to flourish, was the under-investment in public sector foster care. With low allowances and fees as well as poor status and recognition from their local authorities, foster carers expressed increasing levels of dissatisfaction. Early studies (for example, Knapp and Fenyo, 1989) challenged government figures that suggested foster care cost almost eight times less than residential care. Commentators in the late 1980s estimated that foster carers were bearing considerable costs, as much as 50 per cent of their allowances, which were not forthcoming from their fostering agencies. At that time nearly all of these agencies were local authorities.

The current situation seems to have changed little. One working group chaired by the Directors of the Fostering Network and British Association of Adoption and Fostering (BAAF) assessed the amount of additional costs, alongside current levels of expenditure, necessary for fostering across the four countries of the UK (Tapsfield and Collier, 2005). It concluded that considerable increased investment is required to meet service developments related to foster carer fees, training, and general support and associated staff costs. In England for example, existing estimates of the weekly unit costs were £234 for local authority fostering services and £765 for foster care services purchased from IFPs. This study proposed a sum of £633 as necessary for 'effective foster care services' (Tapsfield and Collier, 2005, p.2) in England, thus pitching their estimate closer to the amount paid by IFPs.

The national survey of IFPs found that these agencies were paying foster carers around 50 per cent of the fees charged to local authorities and that as a result they had a potential income worth at least three times that of local authority foster carers (Sellick and Connolly, 2002). Little wonder then that reported levels of satisfaction of IFP foster carers have endured and are significantly higher than those of their local authority peers (Sellick, 1992, Kirton *et al*, 2003). The fees charged by IFPs to local authorities (and reinvested in high foster carer allowances) had begun to force the hands of local authorities or stolen a march on them. If councils would not invest directly in children through foster carer payments, then the IFPs ensured that they did so indirectly through the fees they charged. As a result local authorities were often 'bumped' into exceeding their budgets by paying unplanned IFP rates because of their own placement shortfall. One local authority manager in a recent commissioning study provided a sobering account of this situation when she said:

> I am spending £1.4 million on under 40 IFP placements and £3.2 million on the other 220 kids that we are looking after in house. The sums don't add up and that is what we're up against all the time (Sellick, 2005, p.12).

Ideology and enterprise

Two other phenomena have altered the map of fostering in Britain - a changing ideology within the public sector alongside a growing welfare entrepreneurialism outside it. When combined, these have become a significant force shifting traditional ideas and practices. The hostility towards IFP provision and its staff and carers, expressed by local authority managers and budget holders, is found in the range of accusations made against the IFPs for poaching carers, charging golf course fees and of making a profit opportunity out of children (Sellick and Connolly, 2002, Sellick and Howell, 2003). Similar sentiments have not however been expressed in the literature in respect of the non governmental adoption sector. The first stage report of a contemporary adoption study of services supporting birth relatives and contact confirms that voluntary adoption agencies (VAAs) are a mix of religious, charitable and not-for-profit organisations co-operating with local authorities through the provision of complementary services (Sellick *et al*, 2006). This study found that many local authorities were quick to commission VAAs to provide birth relative support services. By comparison, IFPs were initially perceived as private and profit-seeking, predatory and competitive agencies with no tradition of supplementing public sector child welfare activities. This gulf in attitudes began to narrow. Social workers' experiences of placing children with IFP foster carers and purchasing related services, largely positive government inspections of IFPs, research evidence and, as we shall see below, legal changes began to challenge these perceptions. As the National Survey showed, by 2001 IFPs were recruiting foster carers who had not, nor were likely, to foster for local authorities and were developing innovative services and providing specialist placements often unavailable elsewhere at the time (Sellick and Connolly, 2002). These developments did seem to shift attitudes and practice towards the use of IFPs in many local authorities and, in some, managers began to view IFPs in much the same way as VAAs. They provided a service which was unavailable within the local authority and in so doing allowed those managers to discharge their duties.

The new founders and directors of IFPs, particularly in the face of considerable hostility from their former local authority colleagues, showed a willingness to take risks in setting up the IFPs. As the national survey discovered:

> although the public sector directly underwrites the IFPs, most encountered set-up costs often involving personal investment and risk. There were examples of agencies being established by drawing on redundancy, retirement and inheritance lump sums as well as by business loans (Sellick and Connolly, 2002, p.108).

In order to develop new and improved services for children and young people, these welfare entrepreneurs blended a business approach with a desire to free themselves from what they saw as the mediocrity of public practice and provision. Those that succeeded were followed, as was evident in the national survey (Sellick and Connolly, 2002) and the review conducted by the Social Care Institute for Excellence (SCIE) (Sellick and Howell, 2004), by foster carers transferring from jobs as teachers, social workers, psychologists, youth workers and nurses. These professionals wanted to go 'back to basics' by practising through foster caring, something they considered themselves trained to do, and to do so, on comparable or enhanced salaries.

A particular feature of the IFPs has been their willingness to offer themselves up to independent scrutiny. The early IFPs volunteered for (a largely positive) examination by the Social Services Inspectorate in 1995 (Department of Health, 1995) and the evaluation of the Midland Foster Care Associates (MFCA) in 1997/1998 (Sellick, 1999, Sellick and Connolly, 1999) was probably the first such commissioned scrutiny of an individual IFP. Many IFP directors believed they had little to hide and seemed secure in the knowledge:

> that their ability to recruit and retain experienced foster carers, offer choices of placement for children and provide them with a range of inter-disciplinary services, especially related to schooling and therapy, [was] more than a match for most local authorities (Sellick, 1999, p.12).

Four years later this factor was confirmed when the review commissioned by the Social Care Institute for Excellence (SCIE) found several examples of agencies which had commissioned independent organisations to evaluate their services. The authors of this review noted that 'in a competitive market place a positive evaluation report is a very useful marketing tool' (Sellick and Howell, 2004, p.496). Whatever the motive, this opening up of the books was significant in two major ways. Firstly, this process very clearly caught the policy mood of transparency and accountability and therefore on a strategic level was instrumental in obtaining investment for the IFPs. Secondly, these evaluations had the potential both of informing and improving practice and policy development in fostering agencies across the public as well as independent sectors.

A key to the success of the IFPs is that their directors and managers have been adept at placing themselves on both sides of the political divide. By the mid 1990s IFPs had grown rapidly from the dozen or so teenage placement agencies based in the south east of England in the late 1980s. They were operating far more widely within a Conservative era which required more competition and less regulation within welfare service provision. The IFPs continued to expand after 1997 when early policy changes at the start of the New Labour age required *Best Value* (Department of Health, 2002a) approaches and later an equitable system of regulation and inspection between fostering agencies in the public and independent sectors. Many IFPs were poised, in the right place, at the right time, with the right people, and were therefore 'fit for purpose' in their ability to adapt to a different policy scene. In particular, the Government's additional funding of the public sector was conditional upon the modernisation of local authority practice and services. In the absence or under-development of alternative models, local authorities were often led to emulate those services which had been developed by IFPs. This increased funding, and the new public sector services it brought, did not neutralise those available from IFPs and certainly did not undermine the growth of further independent providers. Sellick (2002) estimated that there were almost as many IFPs as there were local authorities in England. By 2006 there were virtually twice as many IFPs than English local authorities (Sellick, 2006b).

Legal and policy changes:
Opportunities and risks

The Care Standards Act 2000 brought the inspection of, and services provided by, all public and independent fostering agencies into line. These agencies were therefore registered and inspected in the same way: all were required to comply with the National Standards for Fostering Services and the Fostering Services Regulations, 2002 (Cullen and Lane, 2006). In describing the Government's cross-departmental review of provision for young children in 1998, one commentator referred to 'a commitment to the belief that statutory and voluntary agencies working together with a common goal can achieve more than the sum of the individual parts' (Glass, 1999, p.57) as an underlying principle of the new policy direction. Placement selection and related service provision were certainly key examples of this common goal. As the second New Labour term became the third in the mid-2000s, policy shifts towards commissioning children's services, including foster placements, within children's trusts (Department for Education and Skills, 2005b) consolidated the position of the IFPs as pathfinders or pioneers of educational, therapeutic and other service innovations.

Another feature of this new statutory and policy framework only became apparent once the Care Standards Act had been implemented. Its immediate consequences have been significant. The Act empowered all independent (in addition to local authority) fostering agencies to assess and approve foster carers. Previously only voluntary, not for profit, agencies could be delegated these responsibilities by local authorities (Cullen, 2006). Probably because of this, at the time of the National Survey, 80 per cent of IFAs had registered under the previous arrangements as voluntary agencies. Information now available from the Commission for Social Care Inspection (CSCI) in England exposes a striking difference in the status of IFPs between the 'old' and 'new' agencies. In July 2006, 253 agencies were registered as IFPs in England. Thirty three were old IFPs including branches of Barnardos and the NCH and 28 of these had registered as voluntary, not for profit, organisations. The majority 220 IFPs were new and of these 206 were registered as private, for profit, organisations (CSCI, 2006). The implications are clear. There is now a substantial internal market of private sector fostering agencies in England competing with one another for local authority placement contracts.

On the face of it, the Care Standards Act was an exercise in equal opportunities. On the one hand it required all agencies to be accountable in the same way through regulation, inspection and registration and on the other empowered these agencies to assess and approve their own workforce of foster carers. Yet local authorities are usually large and under-funded organisations with extensive and wide-ranging responsibilities far beyond those of the generally smaller and specialist IFPs. The capability of many local authorities to speedily develop services and innovate is therefore curtailed in comparison to most IFPs. The entrepreneurialism which underpinned the growth and success of these agencies is unlikely to diminish. For many, possibly most, outsourcing contracts from local authorities promises a potentially lucrative income stream. The extent and volume of placements and related services Is likely to far exceed those currently available through service level agreements identified in the SCIE review (Sellick and Howell, 2004) and commissioning study (Sellick, 2005).

Welfare reform and new managerialism

There is a growing literature in which a number of social policy commentators discuss how government reform and the practice of 'new managerialism' have changed the face of welfare in Britain. One edited account brings together assessments of the welfare reforms of New Labour's first term of government (Powell, 2002). In one (Brunsdon and May, 2002) the authors distinguish between voluntary and community, and commercial welfare organisations in their evaluation of the government's approach to independent welfare provision. One of these commentators writes elsewhere that 'policy statements and planned initiatives from the current Labour administration suggest that private welfare is set to feature more prominently in the welfare mix of the future and in ways that are unlikely to be undermined by a government of a different political hue' (Brunsdon, 2003, p.189). The increasing use of the non governmental sector and its commercial and community mix appear therefore to constitute a unifying and sustainable ideology within contemporary British politics.

Other writers have used social work as a case study to describe and explain the links between managerialism and the marketisation of welfare in the New Labour age. Harris (1998) traces the development of management models in social work in the UK from bureau professionalism in the late 1970s to 'new managerialism' in the 1990s. Harlow (2004) explores the role of women in British social work within the dual world of post-feminism and new managerialism. Hodgson (2004) conducted a qualitative study to determine the nature of civil society in Wales and its association with the devolved Welsh Assembly. Heffernan (2006) considers the impact of language on social work practice in Britain especially how the term 'service user' rather than 'client' better reflects the imperative for involvement and collaboration. All offer additional insights as we continue to make sense of contemporary, and to predict future, developments in foster care.

In an open welfare market non governmental agencies compete in the delivery of social work services. This means that alternative rather than supplementary services are developed and provided by private and independent welfare agencies with an imperative to raise standards and reduce costs. In order to do so, services have to be managed rather than simply administered, 'in the most cost-effective and efficient manner (where) management methods have been borrowed from the private sector' (Harlow, 2004, p.169). Harris (1998) makes much the same point in his account of the application of the market to state sector social work which was seen as 'inefficient, wasteful and unbusiness-like with a lack of concern for efficiency and value for money' (Harris, 1998, p.852). There was then a firm view that the public sector could be overhauled by private sector methods. Sellick (2006b) challenges this one dimensional view of private practice and uses a number of studies which scrutinised private and manufacturing company management and business techniques to show that key staff were engaged in activities which were more commonly associated with the public sector. The most recent publication of these social policy commentators includes the phrase 'new public management' to describe where we now appear to be in a welfare world of 'working collaboratively across traditional service boundaries' (Heffernan, 2006, p.142). This seems to fit well with both the implementation of children's trusts and the kinds of contracting arrangements identified in the commissioning study (Sellick, 2005, 2006b). However, Hodgson's account of partnerships between the state, civil society and business anticipates an alternative situation in which, apart from its funding role, the state plays no part in service provision 'where the institutions of civil society, in the form of a mix of voluntary associations and the market, form the proper forum for providing welfare' (Hodgson, 2004, p.140).

At the crossroads

So, is this the choice which is emerging for future practice: between a model where local authorities and IFPs, both old and new, collaborate in the shared provision of foster care, or one where the public sector withdraws and simply outsources placement and other service provision from mostly private independent fostering providers? Either way, the place of public sector provision has shifted considerably over the past decade. Although, as some of the research witnesses in the commissioning study (Sellick, 2005) made clear, the practice of purchasing and providing foster care services is met with mixed views by those engaged in this. There remain strong, opposing opinions about the practice of the mixed economy of fostering and these seem to have two main platforms. The first supports those who object to the use of the public purse for private provision. For example, one local authority social worker in the MFCA evaluation commented that the priority of this agency 'was to attract money rather than the good of the child' (Sellick and Connolly, 1999, p.20). Such views endure as illustrated by a local authority manager in the commissioning study (Sellick, 2005) who six year later said her 'concentration is on developing our business' (Sellick, 2005, p.9) rather than in collaborating with a local IFP. However, these expressions were in the minority. The majority of workers and managers across sectors seemed to share the experiences of Swedish social workers and students who found that 'the impact of ideology seems to diminish' (Dellgran and Hojer, 2005, p.57) with the provision of social work and fostering services which they valued and respected. The second platform supports those who apply what they consider to be effective business-like approaches emerging from the previous political era of compulsory competitive tendering. These managers, and they are found in IFPs as well as local authorities, want to do business in the purchase and provision of services as they imagine goods are handled in private and manufacturing companies. The many examples of socio-legal studies which informed the second of the commissioning publications (Sellick, 2006b) challenge this interpretation of doing business.

The Future

Two paths appear to be emerging. In one, which has already been staked out, fostering is being delivered through collaborative arrangements between local authorities and IFPs. These were not always entered into willingly, or voluntarily with good grace and in many local authorities considerable financial problems remain. However, these have become an established feature of the fostering scene. Councils are maintaining a public service in which they approve foster carers, place children and support placements according to their own local capacity. Where this is exceeded, as it generally is, IFPs are commissioned to make up the shortfall in foster placements and related services. Practice varies, but that is the route which is being followed across the country. A second path is at a later stage of construction. At its core is an internal market of largely private, for profit, IFPs accountable to shareholders rather than trustees, competing to provide placements purchased by local authorities. Some IFPs are able to supply considerably more placements and services than at present. Indeed many, buoyed up by the success of their enterprise, are keen to follow this other path. A recently published government commissioned study conducted by a large private sector financial company argues strongly (and virtually uncritically) for this alternative path (PriceWaterhouseCoopers, 2006). In this scene more and more, and eventually most or all, foster placements will be provided by IFPs.

The success of IFPs to position themselves skilfully and strategically according to differing policy imperatives seems unlikely to diminish. No policy maker or manager is likely to disregard the outputs of IFPs in respect of placement provision, services for children and foster carer support and satisfaction. There are other developments also: for example, the recruitment and retention of particular profiles of foster carers such as actively engaged male carers, and those with relevant professional qualifications and experience, which have resulted from IFP innovation and investment over the past decade (Sellick and Howell, 2003, 2004). A weakening or dismissal of ideology in welfare, shared it seems by policy makers and practitioners alike, may well influence the views and actions of the other key players - the managers, directors and budget holders in both public and independent agencies. Some may share the approach of the local authority manager who thought 'there might be a future where the independent provider can exist without being a threat to the local authority' (Sellick, 2005, p.15). Others, including those who are sympathetic with the view that the public sector should move further to the market place, may prefer a future where the existence of local authority fostering agencies is increasingly replaced by an enhanced private child welfare sector. A steady loss of faith in the ability of the public sector to do a good job and a weakening ideological opposition to free markets are likely to strengthen the IFPs. Independent agencies may well consolidate their position as the providers of more and more fostering placements and related services whilst local authorities provide less and commission more.

Outsourcing is likely to suit some large IFPs which have the capacity to provide a substantial volume of placements to local authorities. The PriceWaterhouseCoopers report identified five large IFPs with multi-million pound annual turnovers and many hundreds (in one case 1,500) of foster carers (PriceWaterhouseCoopers, 2006, p.25). However, for other IFPs, both new and old, the perils identified in the American and Australian studies

(Barber, 2002; Unruh and Hodgkin, 2004) may await successful bidders of outsourced contracts. They may have under-estimated their costs in order to undercut their competitors. In so doing, they may have to reduce their services to children and foster carers. Doing the former may jeopardise their ability to recapture contracts when these are reviewed and doing the latter may risk undermining foster carer satisfaction and retention. A former Director of BAAF in Scotland sets out the dangers which voluntary providers have already faced:

> ... while the larger agencies within the sector, such as Barnardos and NCH, have the strength, financial power and wisdom to retain adequate space for innovative projects, smaller agencies are becoming increasingly preoccupied with meeting their contract specifications, with little room for manoeuvre. For these agencies, the barriers to entry into the welfare market have been removed, but the option of exit from the market has also been removed from their control. The result may be stifled growth and lack of innovation (Giltinan, 2002, p.55).

Outsourcing would allow councils to predict and reduce costs by budgeting for large volume based contracts with IFPs. However, beyond the short-term, outsourcing is unlikely to suit local authorities. In the medium and longer terms, financial and supply difficulties may mean that IFPs are unable to deliver the same quality and quantity of services. Outsourcing may simply therefore transfer rather than solve public sector funding problems. Relying on a competitive market place where other IFPs can tender more favourably than those struggling to deliver on the terms of the original contracts will create additional difficulties. Perhaps the greatest of these for local authorities would be the instability and disruption for looked after children being transferred from the foster carers of one IFP to another. In other words, exactly the same problems that New Labour policy initiatives such as *Quality Protects, Best Value,* and *Choice Protects* (Department of Health, 1998, 2002a, Department for Education and Skills, 2005c) were designed to solve.

Conclusion

The provision of foster care in Britain has changed significantly during the last decade although there are some certainties. Fostering is no longer a public sector activity occasionally supplemented by specialist schemes in long-established voluntary child care organisations. The combination of an undersupply of local authority foster carers, and the heavy demand in terms of both volume and needs of the children and young people placed, has ended that virtual monopoly position. The non governmental sector's role in providing foster placements and related therapeutic and educational services has grown significantly, some would say spectacularly, in the past decade. There is no evidence that the mixed economy of foster care provision will improve outcomes for children and young people. Although the range of services for children and young people placed in the IFPs has been valued by their agency foster carers, and the placing local authority social workers, there is virtually no evidence that these services are more successful or that they provide added value, beyond those available within local authorities, or that any such benefit is long-lasting. As Sellick and Connolly say: 'We know that IFA foster carers rate their support services very highly but we do not know whether these make a difference to children' (Sellick and Connolly, 2002, p.119).

For much of the time most of the non-governmental foster care sector comprised voluntary, not for profit agencies, staffed and managed by former local authority social workers. Their identity as innovators and pioneers of services for children and support for foster carers placed them in the tradition of the established voluntary sector. It also led to high levels of expressed satisfaction by the carers attached to these agencies and the social workers commissioning their services. That status has clearly changed. Currently, non governmental fostering agencies are almost exclusively registered as private organisations. Legal changes introduced by the Care Standards Act have enabled this to happen, but ideological changes, shared it seems by many of the key players, have cemented this development. Many welcome it as a sign of enterprise, and wish to support and defend this new position. The consequences are less certain. Researchers and practitioners in Kansas and South Australia (and some distinguished commentators in this country) have strongly cautioned against the drive towards a free foster care market characterised by open and competitive tenders for outsourced contacts (Barber, 2002; Unruh and Hodgkin, 2004; Gittings, 2002). But even if their voices have been heard by those who have the power to slow down or temper this drive, the possibilities of fewer supply difficulties for local authorities and greater demand certainties for IFPs may be too tempting to resist. This is particularly so if these are driven by a political consensus that the market can invigorate a moribund public sector and constrain costs. This position does not necessarily preclude the kinds of collaborative working relationships which have accompanied this new world of inter-sector arrangements, especially if welfare mangers understand that some of their private and manufacturing sector peers have learnt to value and apply these kind of arrangements and relationships. Contracting through co-operation and collaboration may well become the exemplar, even in a more business-minded private welfare sector.

References

Barber, J. (2002) Competitive Tendering and Out-of-Home Care for Children: The South Australian Experience. *Children and Youth Services Review*, 24, 3, 159-174

Brunsdon, E. (2003) Private welfare. in P. Alcock, A. Erskine, and M. May (Eds.) *The Companion to Social Policy.* Oxford, Blackwell

Brunsdon, E. and May, M. (2002) Evaluating New Labour's approach to independent welfare provision. in M. Powell (Ed.) *Evaluating New Labour's Welfare Reforms.* Bristol: The Policy Press

CSCI (Commission for Social Care Inspection) (2006) Independent Fostering Providers. Personal Communication, 7th July 2006, enquiries@csci.gsi.gov.uk. Commission for Social Care Inspection

Cullen, D (2006) Personal Communication, 20th July 2006. Deborah.cullen@baaf. org.uk. British Association for Adoption and Fostering

Cullen, D and Lane, M (2006) *Child Care Law: A summary of the law in England and Wales.* London: BAAF

Dellgran, P. and Hojer, S. (2005) Privatisation as Professionalisation? Attitudes, motives and achievements among Swedish social workers, *European Journal of Social Work*, 8, 1, 39-62

Department for Education and Skills (2005a) *Children Looked After in England, 2004/5.* Statistical Bulletin. London: DfES

Department for Education and Skills. (2005b) *Every Child Matters: Children's Trusts.* Available at www.everychildmatters.gov.uk/aims/childrenstrusts/faq/

Department for Education and Skills (2005c) http://www.dfes.gov.uk/choiceprotects/

Department for Education and Skills (2006) *Care Matters: Transforming the lives of children and young people in care.* London: TSO

Department of Health (1995) *Independent Fostering Agencies Study.* Social Services Inspectorate Report. London: HMSO

Department of Health (1998) *Quality Protects: Transforming Children's Services,* Lomdon, The Stationary Office

Department of Health (2001) Alan Milburn's speech to the Annual Social Services Conference, 19th October

Department of Health (2002a) *Getting the Best from Best Value.* London: Department of Health. Available at www.doh.gov.uk/ssi/gettingbestvalue.htm

Department of Health (2002b) Health Minister announces major review of fostering and placement services. London: Department of Health Media Centre, 19th April

Giltinan, D. (2002) Child care at the end of the millennium. in M. Hill (Ed.) *Shaping Childcare Practice in Scotland.* London: BAAF

Glass, N. (1999) Sure Start: The development of an early intervention programme for young people in the UK. in K. White (Ed.), *Children and Social Exclusion..* London: NCVCCO

Harlow, E. (2004) Why don't women want to be social workers anymore? New managerialism, postfeminism and the shortage of social workers in Social

Services Departments in England and Wales. *European Journal of Social Work,* 7, 2, 167-179

Harris, R. (1998) Scientific Management, bureau-professionalism, new managerialism: the Labour process of state social work. *British Journal of Social Work,* 28, 839-862

Heffernan, K. (2006) Social work, New Public Management and the language of 'Service-User'. *British Journal of Social Work,* 36, 139-147

Hodgson, L. (2004) Manufactured civil society: Counting the cost. *Critical Social Policy,* 24, 2, 139-164

Kirton, D., Ogilvie, K., and Beecham, J. (2003) *Remuneration and Performance in Foster Care,* Department of Health, London

Knapp, M. and Fenyo, A. (1989) Efficiency in foster care: proceeding with caution, in J. Hudson and B. Galaway, (Eds) *The State as Parent.* New York: Kluwer Academic Publishers

Petrie, S. and Wilson, K. (1999) Towards the disintegration of child welfare services. *Social Policy and Administration,* 33, 2, 181-196

Powell, M. (2002) (Ed.) *Evaluating New Labour's Welfare Reforms.* Bristol: The Policy Press

PriceWaterhouseCoopers (2006) *DfES Children's Services, Children's Homes and Fostering.* www.dfes.gov.uk/research/data/uploadfiles/RW74pdf. accessed 06/09/06

Sellick, C. (1992) *Supporting Short Term Foster Carers.* Aldershot: Avebury

Sellick, C. (1999) Independent fostering agencies: Providing high quality services to children and carers? *Adoption and Fostering,* 23, 4, 7-14

Sellick, C. (2002) The aims and principles of independent fostering agencies: A view from the inside. *Adoption and Fostering,* 26, 1, 56-63

Sellick, C. (2005) Opportunities and risks: Models of good practice in commissioning foster care. *British Journal of Social Work,* Advance Access published December 6 2005, pp. 1-15

Sellick, C. (2006a) From famine to feast: A review of the foster care research literature.*Children and Society,* 20, 1, 67-74

Sellick, C. (2006b) Relational contracting between local authorities and independent fostering providers: Lessons in conducting business for child welfare managers. *Journal of Social Welfare and Family Law,* 28, 2, 107-120

Sellick, C. and Connolly J (1999) *A Description and Evaluation of the work of the Midland Foster Care Associates.* Norwich: UEA, Centre for Research on the Child and Family

Sellick, C. and Connolly J. (2001) *National Survey of Independent Fostering Agencies.* Norwich: UEA, Centre for Research on the Child and Family

Sellick, C. and Connolly J. (2002) Independent fostering agencies uncovered: The findings of a national study, *Child and Family Social Work* 7, 2, 107-120

Sellick, C. and Howell, D. (2003) *Innovative, Tried and Tested. A review of good practice in fostering.* [Social Care Institute for Excellence Knowledge Review 4] Bristol: The Policy Press

Sellick, C. and Howell, D. (2004) A description and analysis of multi-sectoral fostering in the United Kingdom. *British Journal of Social Work* 34, 4, 481-499

Sellick, C., Neil, E., Lorgelly, P., Young, J., and Healy, N. (2006) *Supporting the Birth Relatives of Adopted Children and Supporting Post-adoption Contact in Complex Cases: A study of service provision, cost and outcomes.* Stage 1: Service Mapping. [Report to the Department for Education and Skills] Norwich: University of East Anglia

Sellick C., Thoburn, J, and Philpot T. (2004) *What Works in Adoption and Foster Care?* London: Barnardos/BAAF

Swain, V (2005) Campaign Update. *Foster Care* Issue 120. Fostering Network

Tapsfield, R. and Collier, F. (2005) *The Cost of Foster Care: Investing in our children's future.* London: Fostering Network and BAAF

Triseliotis, J., Borland, M., and Hill, M. (2000) *Delivering Foster Care.* London: British Association for Adoption and Fostering, London

Unruh, J. and Hodgkin, D. (2004) The role of contract design in privatization of child welfare services: The Kansas experience. *Children and Youth Services Review* 26, 771-783

Waterhouse, S. (1997) *The Organisation of Fostering Services: A study of the arrangements for delivery of fostering services in England.* London: National Foster Care Association

Wilson, K., Sinclair, I., Taylor, C, Pithouse, A., and Sellick, C (2004) *Fostering success. An exploration of the research literature in foster care.* Bristol: Social Care Institute for Excellence/The Policy Press.

5
Step forward? Step back?
The professionalisation of fostering

Derek Kirton

Introduction

The past three to four decades have witnessed a clearly discernible, if uneven, trend towards professionalisation in foster care, although as we shall see, this term is both controversial and open to different interpretations. While the discourses of the professional domain have been widely used in the fostering literature, there have been few attempts to critically examine these discourses or locate them within wider theoretical frameworks (Corrick, 1999; Wilson and Evetts, 2006). This chapter seeks to build on this body of work by reviewing relevant developments and debates while considering their implications for foster care. Following a brief historical overview and outlining of theoretical perspectives, an account will be given of the principal 'drivers' of professionalisation. Attention will then be focused on some of the 'wicked issues' associated with the hybrid nature of foster care as 'family' and 'work', before a concluding review of contemporary policy developments and future prospects.

At the outset, it is important to acknowledge the diverse and contested meanings of the 'professional' – including its signification of quality, discipline and dedication, detachment, and being paid. In relation to occupations, it has long carried two rather different meanings, the first marking the boundary between the professional and the amateur or volunteer, the second distinguishing between occupations (Freidson, 1988). Both are relevant to foster care, though to date, the former more so than the latter.

Historical background

The historical use of the term professionalisation in relation to foster care can refer both to distinct phases of pioneering change and the wider permeating effects of such changes. It is customary to trace the first recognised wave of professionalisation to the specialist schemes of the 1970s, led by the Kent Family Placement Scheme (Hazel, 1981; Shaw and Hipgrave, 1983). Focused primarily on 'difficult' teenagers, these schemes sought to extend the boundaries of family–based care, through the payment of fees, training and dedicated support from fostering social workers and collaboration with other carers to share ideas and provide mutual help.

During the 1980s, the boundaries drawn between 'professional' and 'mainstream' fostering became increasingly blurred, as criteria changed and features of the specialist schemes came to be more widely adopted throughout fostering services (Triseliotis et al 1995; Verity, 1999). There was also a sea change in attitudes among carers, with overwhelming opposition to payment giving way to clear majority support (Adamson, 1973; Rhodes, 1993). The blurring of boundaries led many local authorities to abandon or re-organise specialist schemes, but this prompted a second wave of professionalisation as some carers, notably in Kent, resisted such moves by setting up their own fostering agencies. The rise of independent fostering providers (IFPs) has been rapid, growing in less than 20 years to around 260 in number and accounting for almost 20 per cent of fostering placements in England (Commission for Social Care Inspection, 2006; Department for Education and Skills (DfES), 2006a). Core features of IFPs have been generous remuneration for carers and strong supports, often including therapeutic and educational services, out of hours provision and greater availability of respite care (Sellick, 2002; Sellick and Connolly, 2002). Due in part to the competition provided by IFPs, these features have been increasingly adopted by local authorities. However, despite these moves towards 'professionalisation', fee payment to foster carers is far from universal, with the Fostering Network (Swain, 2007) estimating that 40 per cent remain effectively unpaid volunteers.

The long-term trend towards 'professionalisation' can also be detected in the policy arena, where central government has become more directive, initially setting a national minimum allowance to cover expenses (albeit regarded as 'derisory' by fostering organisations) and subsequently endorsing fee payments in its Green Paper *Care Matters* (DfES, 2006b). These contemporary policy issues, including the progressive inclusion of carers within the children's workforce, will be discussed later in the article. The government has also supported new 'professional' ventures by adopting models of Treatment Foster Care from the United States of America (USA) and launching Intensive Fostering as a disposal for young offenders (DfES, 2006b).

Theorising the professional domain

Early study of the professional domain revolved around an ideal typical set of 'traits', derived from established professions such as medicine and law (Johnson, 1972; MacDonald, 1995). Although the precise list of traits may vary, the core elements are usually those of specialised knowledge and skills, an ideal of service, license-based monopoly, autonomy, self-regulation and an ethical code (Wilensky, 1964; Moore, 1970). They reflect a tacit bargain between profession and state, whereby the former's skills, ethical practice and devotion to service are recognised by the latter in the form of licensed closure and significant self-regulation. The traits model has been widely used as a benchmark by which to gauge whether occupations merit professional status, with terms such as semi- (or para-)professional coined to describe those meeting some but not all of the criteria. Such epithets have been particularly applied to the 'caring professions' of nursing, social work and teaching, which have been depicted as lacking the necessary specialised knowledge base and autonomy for full professional status (Etzioni, 1969; Toren, 1972). The 'traits' model has also been used to study the process of professionalisation, with Wilensky (1964) for example, identifying the following 'stages' – becoming a full-time occupation, developing training and university based academic qualifications, forming professional associations, certification, gaining monopoly and developing a code of ethics – noting that these have not always been traversed sequentially.

While early studies of the professions tended to accept the 'service ideal' at face value, this changed markedly in the more radical climate of the 1970s and with mounting 'scandals' shaking faith in the competence and ethics of professionals (Foster and Wilding, 2000). Invoking Shaw's description of professions as 'conspiracies against the laity', a series of fierce critiques were launched from both the political left and right. Their common ground was the idea that far from the 'service ideal', professions were primarily concerned with power and self-interest, whether in pursuit of financial gain or their use of self-regulation to avoid genuine accountability. From the radical left, they were depicted as providing career opportunities for the privileged while upholding middle class, patriarchal and ethnocentric values (Larson, 1977; Hearn, 1982; Hugman, 1991). Thus, from a feminist perspective, it was argued that 'semi-professional' status could better be understood as reflecting male control over predominantly female occupations and a broader devaluing of 'women's work' (Witz, 1992).

These critiques made issues of power and struggle central to the study of professions and professionalisation. 'Traits' were to be considered as strategic devices for 'collective mobility projects' (Larson, 1977), while conversely, employers might engage in de-professionalisation, through routinisation, bureaucratisation and other controls over the labour process, a theme taken up in relation to social work by various authors (Howe, 1986; Harris, 2002;

Healy and Meagher, 2004). From a different vantage point, others have argued that the professional quest should be eschewed or reframed in order to bring workers into more equal and empowering relationships with their clients (Illich, 1977; Beresford and Croft, 2001). For their part, theorists of the new right have seen market disciplines, external and internal, and tighter management control as the remedies for unresponsive public sector professionals (Brewer and Lait, 1980; Clarke and Newman, 1997).

A further development in theorising the professional domain has drawn on the work of Foucault to consider professionalism as a disciplinary mechanism for occupational change (Fournier, 1999). This process works through 'technologies of self', encouraging workers to identify with the changes and engage in the required self-development and self-discipline (Aldridge and Evetts, 2003). Collectively, these theoretical perspectives alert us to crucial debates in study of the professional domain. Johnson's (1972) description of the professions as 'Janus-faced' is still applicable today, with positive images of the 'service ideal' co-existing uneasily with more cynical interpretations of their motives and activities..

Explaining professionalisation in foster care

The trend towards professionalisation in foster care can be understood as reflecting several factors arising from changes within foster care and wider contextual developments (see also Wilson and Evetts (2006)). The first relates to the perception that children and young people (hereafter shortened to children) in foster care present greater challenges than ever before. While such sentiments tend to recur in each generation (Adamson, 1973; Pearson, 1983), it remains the case that a higher proportion of looked after children have experienced abuse and neglect, and that the precipitous fall in residential care means relatively more challenging children being placed in foster care. A second relates to changes in the role and tasks of foster carers. Originating in moves from 'exclusive', quasi-adoptive fostering to working 'inclusively' with birth families and social workers (Holman, 1975), these changes accelerated following the Children Act 1989 and its philosophy of 'partnership' with birth families. Thereafter, carers became increasingly involved in contact arrangements and imparting parenting skills (Cleaver, 2000). There was also greater participation in the more formal aspects of the care system, such as attendance at reviews and planning meetings, keeping written records, 'assessing' children, undertaking life story work, or giving evidence in court. Third, foster carers have been subject to tighter monitoring and regulation due both to 'managerialism' and the 'audit culture' and measures to safeguard against child abuse (Kendrick, 1998).

Fourth, the changing role of women in relation to paid work has generated pressure for fostering to provide an income in order to attract and retain carers, an issue to which we return below.

Pressure towards professionalisation has also come from foster carers themselves and their representative bodies. The Fostering Network (and its predecessor organisations) has consistently set out the case for a professional foster care service in manifestos (National Foster Care Association (NFCA), 1989; Fostering Network, 2004) and campaigning documents (NFCA, 1997; Tapsfield and Collier, 2005). It has also played a pivotal role in developing and promoting training programmes for foster carers, from the 1980s *Parenting Plus* through to today's *Skills to Foster* (Lowe, 1999). In relation to payments, the Fostering Network has surveyed local authority allowances against its own recommended minimum allowances, while arguing for reward payments to rest on carers' skills rather than on the difficulties of particular placements. The twin emphases on training and skills-based remuneration came together in the tiered *Payment for Skills* model in the 1990s (NFCA, 1993).

Wilson and Evetts (2006) argue that professionalisation has taken place largely 'from above', as a means of securing occupational change, and in Miller and Rose's (1990) phrase 'control at a distance'. The argument advanced here, however, is that this underestimates the part played by organisations such as the Fostering Network (and local associations) in creating pressure 'from below'. While the local histories have gone largely unrecorded, the Fostering Network's campaigns and activities have promoted a clear and coherent vision of professional foster care and represented carers' aspirations to policy-makers. It has also provided specific proposals such as the *Payment for Skills* model which has been widely adopted by local authorities and effectively endorsed in the recent Green Paper (DfES, 2006b). Moreover, the Fostering Network has played a prominent role in policy formulation, for example in the development of national standards for foster care (UK Joint Working Party on Foster Care, 1999; Department of Health, 2002).

The professionalising trend in foster care can also be understood as part of a broader emergence, especially under New Labour, of the 'social investment state' (Giddens, 1998) with its targeting of welfare spending towards global competitiveness, and focus on early intervention to raise educational attainment and prevent anti-social behaviour (Fawcett et al, 2004). This focus has included efforts to professionalise groups such as childminders (Bostock, 2003) and play workers (Cameron et al, 2003). The twin concerns of investment and combating social exclusion create a powerful context for a focus on looked after children, who past and present, have been linked to a variety of social problems including educational failure, unemployment, homelessness, substance abuse, early parenthood and crime (Chief Secretary to the Treasury, 2003).

The 'social investment state' has brought a blurring of the boundary between public and private spheres, with responsibilities shifting in both directions between state and family (Meyer, 2000; Daly and Lewis, 2003). This has included a general trend towards 'professionalisation' for carers and parents, comprising a mixture of setting standards and codification, provision of support, training and in some instances, financial incentives (Henderson and Forbat, 2002; Henricson, 2003; Gillies, 2005). There have also been moves towards recognition of 'lay expertise', manifest in ideas about the expert patient, the expert carer, or even, in the case of parents of disabled children, the role of lead *professional* (emphasis added) (Kirk and Glendinning, 2002. Children Now, 27.9.06, News, p.4). While it could be argued that such developments make it more difficult to distance fostering from 'ordinary parenting', they also facilitate recognition of expertise arising from close relationships rather than academic credentials.

Collectively, the factors discussed above have generated a strong and growing momentum towards professionalisation. However, this path remains a rocky one for a number of reasons, referred to here as 'wicked issues' to reflect their deep and enduring nature.

Professionalisation in foster care:
The wicked issues

Love and money

The complex relationship between love and money has lain at the heart of many debates regarding professionalisation in foster care. Such debates revolve around two conflicting paradigms. One posits an essential contradiction between personal relationships built on emotional ties and the cash-nexus of the labour market. The influence of the latter is seen as corrosive, leading to an instrumental and impersonal approach to care work (Zelizer, 1997; Folbre and Nelson, 2000). However, it has been argued that this dualism is over-simplified and misleading (Land, 2002). For example, research suggests that rather than being reduced to the values of economic exchange, paid care work is often characterised by close personal relationships (Stone, 2000). Nelson (1999) similarly questions prevailing notions of 'self-interest' and 'mercenary motivation' in working 'for the money', suggesting that paid care work may be done to provide (necessities) for others. She also contends that the romanticisation of altruism rests heavily on gendered assumptions about women's self-sacrifice, and that its association with the private sphere may mask more complex motives and power dynamics (see also Pahl, 1989). Folbre and Nelson (2000) argue that 'commodification' is not simply a product of monetary exchange, but depends on the diverse meanings attached to flows of money, for example whether it is perceived as controlling or acknowledging.

The second paradigm sees no necessary conflict between pecuniary and non-pecuniary values and focuses on the incentive effect of remuneration and its capacity to 'value' activities. This may be expressed pejoratively, as in references to foster carers being paid 'less than it costs to keep a dog in a kennel' (Colton and Williams, 2006 p.115) or in more measured recognition of the importance of market values in our society (Triseliotis et al, 1995). Advocates of professionalisation may also ask why the concerns raised regarding foster carers' motivations are not applied to others working with children, for example social workers or psychologists (Verity, 1999).

Such arguments are persuasive to a degree, but do not entirely address the distinctive nature of relationships within fostering and the importance of carers' personal commitment, whether as an antidote to a bureaucratic and otherwise 'uncaring' system (Sergeant, 2006), or the development of attachments and possibilities of permanence (Schofield et al, 2000). Nutt talks of carers' 'vocabulary of emotionality' (2006, p.80) and how they constructed themselves as 'intimately connected to the children' (2006 p.74), regarding this as crucial in improving the latter's lives. This does not, of course, mean that commitment should be exploited or that foster carers should be financially 'penalised' for their importance to children. However, it does suggest that there are vital elements to fostering that may be at risk if professionalisation is implemented in a way that encourages 'calculative' approaches to care. However complex the term, 'altruism' remains an important part of foster care (Sinclair et al, 2004)

Family and work

The location of foster care in relation to 'family' and 'work' is relevant to professionalisation both in its passage from voluntarism and its quest for the status of profession. In ideal typical form, these domains are assumed to operate quite differently, resting on emotional bonds and contractual exchange respectively. For foster care, this generates two competing benchmarks for comparison, namely those of 'ordinary (or adoptive) parenting' and residential child care. As in the case of love and money, however, these dichotomies can be problematised, especially in the light of feminist scholarship emphasising (domestic and care) *work* within the family and the importance of emotions within paid labour (Hochschild, 1983; Parry et al, 2005). The shift towards goal-oriented placements (e.g. reunification and so forth), the wide range of tasks outlined earlier and in some instances, therapeutic or treatment roles have drawn foster care closer to conceptualisation as 'work'. One obvious sign of the shift has been the change of nomenclature from foster *parent* to foster *carer*. In turn, this has been strengthened by attempts to resolve 'status' problems in areas such as taxation and pension entitlements (Her Majesty's Revenue and Customs, 2005). Meanwhile, at local levels, greater attention has been devoted to 'terms and conditions', for example paid holiday entitlements.

Yet despite this broad trend, it can be argued that foster care remains characterised by hybridity, not least because much of the 'work' of fostering is carried out in and through the family, with a relative absence of temporal and spatial separation. This, in turn, means that the normative 'privacy' of the family must be managed in conjunction with the bureaucracy and external surveillance associated with the care system. Particular challenges include how to treat foster children (perhaps with formal entitlements to pocket money or clothing allowances) and the carers' own children. (Kirton, 2001). Similarly, the impact of abuse allegations or risks associated with theft, damage, or violence from foster children or their families are likely to be experienced directly within the foster family (Nixon, 1997).

In the context of work, hybridity poses two distinct challenges. First, the boundaries between work and non-work are open to widely divergent interpretations. Oldfield (1997) calculated the former in terms of the 'additional' demands arising from fostering, estimating these at around 13-14 hours per week. Alternatively, foster care may be viewed as a '24/7' or '365 day' job, a stance favoured by advocates of professionalisation, but perhaps exaggerating the impact of a foster child's presence or pervasion of a 'work ethos' in the context of family life. A second related challenge is that of how foster carers see their role. Research findings suggest that rather than regarding parenting and job as alternatives, many foster carers draw simultaneously on both discourses. Thus, although typically at least two thirds of carers endorse the idea of fostering as a job meriting payment, they are still more likely to describe their role in terms of parenting than as a worker or professional (Hayden et al, 1999; Kirton et al, 2003).

Within this hybridity, there are of course, invisible boundaries surrounding 'family', perhaps most clearly apparent when placements or fostering careers are ended because of perceived adverse affects on family members, but also when foster children move progressively from 'outsider' to 'insider' status, permanence or even adoption. Irrespective of longer term outcomes, these boundaries are also important in terms of emotional integration and sense of belonging for foster children.

The relationship between hybridity and professionalisation is a complex one. Initially, the professionalising trend was focused on cultivating greater detachment, so that carers would be 'concerned but not possessive' (Parker ADD DATE, cited Adamson, 1973). However, the danger that detachment might mean a loss of emotional involvement and commitment has long been recognised (Dinnage and Kellmer Pringle, 1967) and is reflected in Nutt's (2006) call for 'detached attachment'. Achieving this is perhaps especially challenging in longer term or permanent placements where detachment might be seen as a barrier to the development of deeper emotional ties or when professionalism is associated with therapeutic skills and change.

Knowledge, skills and training

As outlined above, the development of knowledge and skills are central to professionalisation, and in the case of foster care, this has been manifested in a steady growth in training (Lowe, 1999). Its content reflects both issues relating directly to foster children within the family and broader 'system' issues (for typical ranges of topics see e.g. Triseliotis et al, 2000, p.74-5 or Sinclair et al, 2004, p.112). Focusing initially on preparatory courses, this was subsequently extended to post-approval training. The first National Vocational Qualification (NVQ) for fostering was introduced in 1996 and qualification at Level 3 has become the widely accepted benchmark target for carers at national and local levels. Beyond this level, there have also been tentative efforts to develop qualifications linked to higher education (Sellick and Howell, 2003). Training has been important as a means of marking distance from 'ordinary parenting' and in turn justifying other aspects of the professionalising project, including remuneration, with qualifications often recognised financially, either directly, or indirectly as a criterion within tiered schemes

However, if training has become an established feature of foster care, its present scope remains limited, especially in relation to stronger professionalising ambitions. Despite expectations that all foster carers participate in post-approval training, attendance has been found to be highly variable, with relatively weak sanctions in the case of non-attendance (presumably explicable in terms of reluctance to lose carers or disrupt placements) (Farmer et al, 2004). Meanwhile, in relation to NVQ level 3, Tapsfield and Collier (2005) estimated that only 5 per cent of foster carers had attained this marker. Cameron and Boddy (2006) are also critical of what they term the vocational-industrial approach of the NVQ and advocate moving to a more professional model represented by the social pedagogue, with its emphasis on skills underpinned by theoretical knowledge. This could, in principle, form the basis of training for at least some foster carers, but this remains a distant prospect at present. While research on the effectiveness of training is in its infancy, there is to date little evidence of a link between training and child outcomes although there may be indirect benefits in terms of feelings of support and engagement with fostering as well as retention (Minnis and Devine, 2001; Pithouse et al, 2002; Macdonald and Kakavelakis, 2004; Sinclair et al, 2004).

The hybrid nature of foster care may also give rise to tensions over the value placed on what Cameron and Boddy (2006) term tacit knowledge, derived from life experience and practice wisdom. Tacit knowledge figures prominently in recruitment and initial approval and arguably remains crucially important to successful fostering. It is therefore important both that formal training complements rather than undermines tacit knowledge and that capable carers are not unduly penalised due to lack of formal qualifications.

Professionalisation, homogeneity and differentiation among foster carers

The professionalising trend relates not only to the broader parameters of foster care but its 'internal' constitution. To the extent that professionalisation reflects and reinforces distance from 'ordinary parenting', the diverse types of fostering generate pressures to differentiate between carers. Seen most dramatically in the distinction between 'professional' and 'mainstream' fostering, this is also implicit within tiered systems and in differences of payment and training requirements attached to particular schemes. Differentiation along an axis from family/voluntary to professional has also been seen as a means of accommodating carers with different orientations (Adamson, 1973; Hudson, 1999). However, there are also forces resisting differentiation, including a reluctance to create 'second class' carers or children, recognition of the unpredictable nature of placement 'difficulty', or notions that demands may be 'different but equal' (for example between short- and long-term placements).

Arguably the most vexatious aspect of differentiation has related to family and friends as carers (FFAC), an increasingly favoured placement option (Farmer and Moyers, 2005). Historically, FFAC have often been paid at lower rates (or not at all) but in recent times, the trend has been towards equalisation, driven by legal challenges to discrimination as well as broader advocacy for this placement option (Broad, 2001; Gillen, 2004). Equalisation, however, sits uneasily within a professionalising framework. Typically, the perceived strengths of FFAC are those of continuity, familiarity, attachment and identity rather than their 'generic' skills. Indeed, it is widely acknowledged that many would not be approved as carers for children outside the family (Wheal, 1999). Similarly, arguments for payment tend to emphasise opportunity costs and levels of need for FFAC, many of whom have low incomes (Waterhouse, 2001). It is also clear that many (probably a majority of) FFAC do not identify themselves with the professionalising project, including the requirement for training in order to look after a grandchild or understand the workings of the child care system (O'Brien, 2000; Tapsfield, 2001). The recent Green Paper (DfEs, 2006b) has acknowledged this uneasy relationship by proposing revision to assessment processes and support for FFAC to recognise the probability that they will only ever care for one child.

Professionalisation in foster care: 'Progress' and prospects

The current state and future direction of the professionalising project in foster care can be considered both in terms of feasibility and desirability. Though it has a considerable history, the trend towards professionalisation has shown signs of acceleration. In pursuit of its aim of 'improving the number and quality of foster carers', the Green Paper (DfES 2006b) incorporates four main measures relevant to professionalisation. The first, and arguably most important is the proposal to introduce 'a tiered framework of placements to respond to different levels of need' (p.7). Despite this use of the language of need, accompanying references to corresponding fees, skills and career progression for foster carers all suggest that the framework will be very similar to the *Payment for Skills* model. Second, this is to be underpinned by a new qualifications framework, including the development of (foundation) degrees in foster care (p.49). A third proposal is that of mandatory registration for foster carers, and in that regard placing them on an equal footing with social workers and residential workers. Finally, inclusion of foster carers within the children's workforce is clearly endorsed (Campbell, 2005), including their possible treatment as 'key workers' for housing purposes. Even without additional funding for implementation, there is no doubting the shift away from voluntarism and it could be argued that professionalisation, in its 'occupational' sense, is clearly on the horizon.

In its second meaning, attaining the status of a 'profession', there is rather more, and more controversial, ground to traverse. Beyond the Green Paper proposals for (foundation) degrees, opportunities for foster carers arise from two sources: first the promotion of social pedagogy (see above); and second the weakening of traditional boundaries as commonalities within the children's workforce are emphasised (Chief Secretary to the Treasury, 2003). However, there remain significant challenges in raising qualification levels from their current low base, including lack of entry qualifications, busy lives, career plans and turnover. At present, the prospect of a substantial 'graduate' element within foster care remains somewhat distant.

Autonomy and discretion are also important elements with the professional domain and here foster care represents something of a paradox. On the one hand, carers have considerable autonomy in terms of day-to-day living and how to deal with their foster children. Conversely, however, this takes place within a framework where the major decisions are taken by others and even relatively minor decisions may be subject to bureaucratic controls (although there has been some recent relaxation in respect of carers' powers to approve foster children's overnight stays with friends). As Hugman (1991) observes, occupational claims are always judged in the context of the professional claims and status of other groupings and for foster carers, social workers are clearly the most important of these. Corrick

(1999) has suggested that social workers' shaky professsional status makes them more reluctant to recognise foster carers as professionals. However, it can be argued that the delegation of tasks (such as life story work or liaison with schools) may enhance social workers' professional status so long as they remain in supervisory charge (Triseliotis et al, 1995). In the absence of organisational and cultural change, narrowing any status gap between foster carers and social workers is likely to prove difficult, due to a mix of respective qualification levels, vested legal powers, historical legacy and the significant personal scrutiny to which foster carers are subjected.

Some of the challenges of professionalisation are catered for within a tiered model, which allows the more 'professionally oriented' carers to seek progression and arguably greater potential to participate fully within decision-making. In effect, it allows for differences, without the binarism of professional and mainstream. It is unclear at present, however, if specialist schemes such as those relating to remand, treatment foster care or intensive fostering will operate outside the tiered model.

The desirability of professionalisation in foster care clearly raises questions of 'desirable for whom?' and according to what criteria. The case for professionalisation and greater investment in the foster care system has a strong plausibility (Tapsfield and Collier, 2005), but is far from proven. Evidence of improved child outcomes has come primarily from evaluations of professional schemes with troubled adolescents (see e.g. Caesar et al, 1994; Chamberlain and Reid, 1998; Testa and Rolock, 1999) but it is debateable how far these findings might apply to other types of fostering. Wider research has identified certain carer characteristics - notably personal qualities such as warmth, resilience and empathy, or parenting styles based on encouragement – as ingredients for successful foster care (Berridge and Cleaver, 1987; Sinclair and Wilson, 2003; Farmer et al, 2004). To the author's knowledge, however, there has been no research relating such characteristics (or child outcomes) to professional orientations or levels of training. There is also need for research to explore the relationship between professionalisation and recruitment and retention, where the evidence remains limited and somewhat inconclusive (Waterhouse, 1997; Kirton et al, 2003). Similarly, despite the obvious sensitivities, there is a need for more research on children's perspectives on professionalisation.

Thus, in terms of securing improved performance, the proposed professionalising measures of the Green Paper still represent something of an act of faith. Beyond government rhetoric, however, there is a strong case for professionalisation on grounds of social justice and gender equality. There is little doubt that historically the work of foster carers has been, and for many continues to be, exploited and that this work is still predominantly undertaken by women (Smith, 1988; Rhodes, 1993; Nutt, 2006). Setting aside debates regarding the transformation or reinforcement of gender roles, professionalisation does offer female carers some redress as well as representing a pragmatic adaptation to the social norms of working mothers and two income families. It remains to be seen, however, whether professionalising measures will increase the supply of families willing and able to take on what is both a very distinctive lifestyle and challenging work.

Concluding discussion

Despite its unevenness, the professionalising trend within foster care over recent decades is unmistakeable. An attempt has been made here to contribute to an as yet small, but growing debate regarding the professionalising process. While endorsing much of the analysis of Wilson and Evetts (2006), it has been argued here that their focus on change 'from above' under-estimates the part played by organisations such as the Fostering Network. This chapter has also emphasised the importance of wider policy contexts and the distinctive 'hybridity' of foster care.

In addressing the 'balance sheet' aspect of the chapter's title, professionalisation in foster care can be seen as a step forward in various important respects. First, it has been pivotal in the extension of 'fosterability', offering family experiences to children whose behaviours and emotional difficulties would once have precluded this. Second, it has played a similar role in work to improve the planning and goal orientation of public care, including the recent efforts to raise the educational attainments of looked after children. Third, the professional focus on performance has facilitated the development of a wide range of services and training provision to support such efforts. Finally, as discussed above, the professionalising trend can be viewed as adaptive to changing social norms and as reducing gender inequality and exploitation in fostering.

However, it is also possible to identify less positive aspects of the process. For some, this would include the demise of voluntarism, which might be seen, if only in an 'ideal world', as the preferred basis for fostering. Earlier discussion of the 'wicked issues' in foster care suggests that while hybridity permits the management of complex and often contradictory principles, it also entails delicate balancing acts. Both in policy and practice terms, there is a danger that over-emphasis on the professional domain, its rationale and requirements, may lead to a loss of the familial. This risk is heightened with increasing prescription and contractualism, whether rooted in ' terms and conditions' or orientation. In the words of one child 'It is not like a family. It's like a staff team' (Sinclair et al, 2005). As noted above, the idea that further professionalisation will improve child outcomes remains somewhat speculative. What is known, however, is that the personal qualities of carers and 'chemistry' involved in foster placements are crucial and should not be undermined. Professionalisation can take different forms and it is vital that it is implemented in a way that manages and nurtures the hybridity of foster care.

References

Adamson, G. (1973) *The Care-Takers.* London: Bookstall

Aldridge, M. and Evetts, J. (2003) Rethinking the concept of professionalism: The case of journalism, *British Journal of Sociology,* 54, 4, 547-64

Beresford, P. and Croft, S. (2001) Service users' knowledges and the social construction of social work. *Journal of Social Work,* 1, 3, 295-316

Berridge D. and Cleaver, H. (1987) *Foster Home Breakdown.* Oxford: Blackwell

Bostock, L. (2003) *Childminding Registration and Private Fostering.* Bristol: Social Care Institute for Excellence

Broad, B. (2001) *Kinship Care: The placement choice for children and young people.* Lyme Regis: Russell House

Brewer, C. and Lait, J. (1980) *Can Social Work Survive?* London: Temple Smith

Caesar, G., Parchment, M and Berridge, D. (1994) *Black Perspectives on Services for Children in Need.* Barkingside, Essex: Barnardos/National Children's Bureau

Cameron, C., Candappa, M., McQuail, S., Mooney, A., Moss, P and Petrie, P. (2003) *Early Years and Childcare International Evidence Project.* London: Thomas Coram Research Unit

Cameron, C. and Boddy, J. (2006) Knowledge and education for care workers: What do they need to know?. in J. Boddy, C. Cameron and P. Moss *Care Work: Present and future.* London: Routledge

Campbell, M. (2005) *Integrated and Qualified: Workforce development for effective delivery of services to vulnerable children and young people and those who care for them. Policy drivers update.* Leeds: Skills for Care

Chamberlain, P. and Reid, J. (1998) Comparison of two community alternatives to incarceration, for chronic juvenile offenders. *Journal of Consulting and Clinical Psychology,* 66, 4, 624-33

Chief Secretary to the Treasury (2003) *Every Child Matters.* Cm5860. London: TSO

Children Now (2006) News. 27 September, p.4

Clarke, J. and Newman, J. (1997) *The Managerial State: Power, politics and ideology in the remaking of social welfare.* London: Sage

Cleaver, H. (2000) *Fostering Family Contact.* London: TSO

Commission for Social Care Inspection (2006) *The State of Social Care*

2005-6. London: Commission for Social Care Inspection

Colton, M. and Williams, M. (Eds.) (2006) *Global Perspectives on Foster Family Care.* Lyme Regis: Russell House

Corrick, H. (1999) The professionalisation of foster care. in A. Wheal *The RHP Companion to Foster Care.* Lyme Regis: Russell House

Daly, M. and Lewis, J. (2003) The concept of social care and the analysis of contemporary welfare states. *British Journal of Sociology,* 51, 2, 281-298

Department for Education and Skills (2006a) *Statistics of Education: Children looked after by local authorities year ending 31 march 2005. Volume 1: National tables.* London: Department for Education and Skills

Department for Education and Skills (2006b) *Care Matters: Transforming the lives of children and young people in care. (Cm 6932).* London: Department for Education and Skills

Department of Health (2002) *Fostering Services: National Minimum Standards, Fostering Services Regulations.* London: TSO

Dinnage, R. and Kelmer Pringle, M. (1967) *Foster Home Care, Facts and fallacies: A review of research in the United States, Western Europe, Israel and Great Britain between 1948 and 1966.* London: Longmans

Etzioni, A. (1969) *Semi-Professions and their Organisation: Teachers, nurses and social workers.* New York: Free Press

Farmer, E., Moyers, S. and Lipscombe, J. (2004) *Fostering Adolescents.* London: Jessica Kingsley

Farmer, E. and Moyers, S. (2005) Children Placed with Family and Friends: Placement patterns and outcomes. Briefing. www.bristol.ac.uk/sps/downloads/Hadley/kinship%20care.doc

Fawcett, B., Featherstone, B., and Goddard, J (2004) *Contemporary Child Care: Policy and practice.* Basingstoke: Palgrave

Folbre, N. and Nelson, J. (2000) For love or money: Or both?. *Journal of Economic Perspectives,* 14, 4, 123–40

Fostering Network (2004) *Survey of Carers.* London: Fostering Network

Foster, P. and Wilding, P. (2000) Whither welfare professionalism? *Social Policy and Adminisration,* 34, 2, 143-59

Fournier, V. (1999) The appeal to 'professionalism' as a disciplinary mechanism. *Sociological Review,* 47, 2, 280-307

Freidson, E. (1988) *Professional Powers: A study in the institutionalisation of formal knowledge.* Chicago: Chicago University Press

Giddens, A. (1998) *Third Way: The renewal of social democracy.* Cambridge: Polity

Gillen, S. (2004) Court action will test discriminatory fostering payments to kinship carers. *Community Care,* 4th March, pp.18-19

Gillies, V. (2005) Meeting Parents' needs? Discourses of 'support' and 'inclusion' in family policy. *Critical Social Policy,* 25, 1, 70-90

Harris, J. (2002) *The Social Work Business.* London: Routledge

Hayden, C., Goddard, J., Gorin, S., and van der Spek, N. (1999) *State Child*

Care: Looking after children?. London: Jessica Kingsley

Hazel, N., (1981) *A Bridge to Independence.* Oxford: Basil Blackwell

Healy, K. and Meagher, G. (2004) The reprofessionalization of social work: Collaborative approaches for achieving professional recognition. *British Journal of Social Work,* 34, 2, 243-60

Hearn, J. (1982) Notes on patriarchy, professionalisation and the semi-professions. *Sociology,* 16, 2, 184-202

Henderson, J. and Forbat, L. (2002) Relationship-based social policy: personal and policy constructions of 'care'. *Critical Social Policy,* 22, 4, 669-687

Henricson, C. (2003) *Government and Parenting: Is there a case for a policy review and a parents' code.* York: Joseph Rowntree Foundation

HM Revenue and Customs (2005) *Foster Care Relief.* www.hmrc.gov.uk/individuals/foster-care-relief.pdf

Hochschild, A. (1983) *The Managed Heart: Commercialisation of human feelings.* Berkely: University of California Press

Holman, R. (1975) The place of fostering in social work. *British Journal of Social Work,* 5, 1, 3-29

Howe, D. (1986) *Social Workers and their Practice in Welfare Bureaucracies.* Aldershot: Gower

Hudson, J. (1999) Summary. in A. Wheal *The RHP Companion to Foster Care.* Lyme Regis: Russell House

Hugman, R. (1991) *Power in Caring Professions.* Basingstoke: Macmillan

Illich, I. (1977) *Disabling Professions.* London: Marion Boyars

Johnson, T. (1972) *Power and Professions.* London: Macmillan

Kendrick, A. (1998) In their best interest? Protecting children from abuse in residential and foster care. *International Journal of Child and Family Welfare,* 3, 2, 169-185

Kirk, S. and Glendinning, C. (2002) Supporting 'expert' parents: Professional support and families caring for a child with complex health care needs in the community, *International Journal of Nursing Studies,* 39, 6, 625-635

Kirton, D. (2001) Family budgets and public money: spending fostering payments. *Child and Family Social Work,* 6, 4, 305-314

Kirton, D., Beecham, J. and Ogilvie, K. (2003) *Remuneration and Performance in Foster Care.* Canterbury: University of Kent

Land, H. (2002) Spheres of care in the UK: separate and unequal, *Critical Social Policy,* 22, 1, 13-22

Larson, M.S. (1977) *The Rise of Professionalism: A sociological analysis.* Berkely: University of California Press

Lowe, K.(1999) Training for foster carers. in A. Wheal *The RHP Companion to Foster Care.* Lyme Regis: Russell House

MacDonald, K. (1995) *The Sociology of the Professions.* London: Sage

Macdonald, G. and Kakavelakis, I. (2004) *Helping Foster Carers to Manage Challenging Behaviour: Evaluation of a cognitive-behavioural training programme for foster carers.* Exeter: University of Exeter, Centre for

Evidence-based Social Services

Meyer, M.H. (2000) *Care Work: Gender, labor and the welfare state.* New York: Routledge

Miller, P. and Rose, N. (1990) Governing economic life. *Economy and Society,* 19, 1, 1-31

Minnis, H. and Devine, C. (2001) The effect of foster carer training on the emotional and behavioural functioning of looked after children. *Adoption and Fostering,* 25, 1, 44-54

Moore, W. (1970 *The Professions: Roles and rules.* New York: Russell Sage Foundation

National Foster Care Association (1989) *Foster Care Charter.* London: National Foster Care Association

National Foster Care Association (1993) *Foster Carers: Payment for skills.* London: National Foster Care Association

National Foster Care Association (1997) *Foster Care in Crisis: A call to professionalise the forgotten service.* London: National Foster Care Association

Nelson, J. (1999) Of markets and martyrs: Is it ok to pay well for care?. *Feminist Economics,* 5,3, 43-59

Nixon, S. (1997) The limits of support in foster care. *British Journal of Social Work,* 27, 6, 913-930

Nutt, L. (2006) *The Lives of Foster Carers: Private sacrifices, public restrictions.* Abingdon: Routledge

O'Brien, V. (2000) Relative care. in G. Kelly and R. Gilligan *Issues in Foster Care: Policy, practice and research,* London: Jessica Kingsley

Oldfield, N. (1997) *The Adequacy of Foster Care Allowances.* Aldershot: Ashgate

Pahl, J. (1989) *Money and Marriage.* Basingstoke: Macmillan

Parker, R. (1966) *Decision in Child Care: A study of prediction in fostering.* London: Allen and Unwin

Parry, J., Taylor, R., Pettinger, L., and Glucksmann, M. (2005) Confronting the challenges of work today: New horizons and perspectives. *Sociological Review,* 53, s2, 1-18

Pearson, G. (1983) *Hooligan: A history of respectable ideas.* London: Macmillan

Pithouse, A., Hill-Tout, J.. and Lowe, K. (2002) Training foster carers in challenging behaviour: A case study in disappointment?. *Child and Family Social Work,* 7, 3, 203-214,

Rhodes, P. (1993) Charitable vocation or 'proper job'?: The role of payment in foster care. *Adoption and Fostering,* 17, 1, 8-13

Schofield, G., Beek, M., and Sargent, K. with Thoburn, J. (2000) *Growing Up in Foster Care.* London: British Agencies for Adoption and Fostering

Sellick, C. (2002) The aims and principles of independent fostering agencies: A view from the inside. *Adoption and Fostering,* 26, 1, 56-63

Sellick, C. and Connolly, J. (2002) Independent fostering agencies uncovered: The findings of a national study. *Child and Family Social Work*, 7, 1, 107-120

Sellick, C. and Howell, D. (2003) *Innovative, Tried and Tested: A review of good practice in fostering.* London: Social Care Institute for Excellence

Sergeant, H. (2006) *Handle With Care: An investigation into the care system.* London: Centre for Young Policy Studies

Shaw, M. and Hipgrave, T. (1983) *Specialist Fostering,* London: Batsford

Sinclair, I. and Wilson, K. (2003) Matches and mismatches: The contribution of carers and children to the success of foster placements. *British Journal of Social Work*, 33, 7, 871-884

Sinclair, I, Gibbs, I., and Wilson, K. (2004) *Foster Carers: Why they stay and why they go.* London: Jessica Kingsley

Sinclair, I, Gibbs, I. and Wilson, K. (2005) *Foster Placements: Why they succeed and why they fail.* London: Jessica Kingsley

Smith, B. (1988) Something you do for love: The question of money and foster care. *Adoption and Fostering*, 12, 4, 34-38

Stone, D. (2000) Caring by the book. in M.H. Meyer *Care Work: Gender, Labor and the Welfare State.* New York: Routledge

Swain, V. (2007) *Can't Afford to Foster: A survey of fee payments to foster carers.* London: Fostering Network

Tapsfield, R. (2001) Kinship care: A family rights group perspective. in B. Broad *Kinship Care: The placement choice for children and young people.* Lyme Regis: Russell House

Tapsfield, R. and Collier, F. (2005) *The Cost of Foster Care: Investing in our children's future.* London: British Agencies for Adoption and Fostering/ The Fostering Network

Testa, M. and Rolock, N. (1999) Professional foster care: A future worth pursuing? *Child Welfare*, 78, 1, 108-124

Toren, N. (1972) *Social Work: The case of a semi-profession.* London: Sage

Triseliotis, J., Sellick C. and Short, R. (1995) *Foster Care: Theory and practice.* London: Batsford/British Agencies for Adoption and Fostering

Triseliotis, J., Borland, M., and Hill, M. (2000) *Delivering Foster Care,* London: British Agencies for Adoption and Fostering

UK Joint Working Party on Foster Care (1999) *UK National Standards for Foster Care.* London: National Foster Care Association

Verity, P. (1999) Financial matters. in A. Wheal *The RHP Companion to Foster Care.* Lyme Regis: Russell House

Waterhouse, S. (1997) *The Organisation of Fostering Services: A study of the arrangements for the delivery of fostering services in England.* London: National Foster Care Association

Waterhouse, S. (2001) Keeping children in kinship placements within court proceedings. in B. Broad *Kinship Care: The placement choice for children and young people.* Lyme Regis: Russell House

Wheal, A. (1999) Family and friends who are carers. in A. Wheal *The RHP Companion to Foster Care.* Lyme Regis: Russell House

Wilensky, H. (1964) Professionalisation of everyone, *American Journal of Sociology,* 70, 2, 137-58

Wilson, K. and Evetts, J. (2006) The professionalisation of foster care. *Adoption and Fostering,* 30, 1, 39-47

Witz, A. (1992) *Professions and Patriarchy.* London: Routledge

Zelizer, V. (1997) *The Social Meaning of Money: Pin money, pay checks, poor relief and other currencies.* Princeton: Princeton University Press

6
Fostering matters:
A foster carer's perspective

Elizabeth Harlow and Foluke Blackburn

Introduction

The authors' of this chapter participated in the symposium 'Fostering Matters' which took place at the University of Salford in March 2007. Elizabeth co-ordinated the event on behalf of the Fostering Network and the journal *Social Work and Social Sciences Review,* whilst Foluke was invited to attend and contribute to the discussion on the grounds of her extensive experience as a social work professional and educator, adoptive parent and foster carer. Foluke, as an experienced social work practitioner, is currently employed as a Lecturer at the University of Salford, and has primary responsibility for educating child care social workers. In addition, she has assessed and trained foster carers. Given the above, however, she has also been a 'service user' in relation to these processes.

The symposium was a stimulating event, but there was inadequate time for discussion. In consequence, conversation on the key themes and the attendant issues for foster carers continued amongst participants for some time afterwards. In order that Foluke's insights as a foster carer were not excluded from the forum of the journal pages, Elizabeth taped and transcribed one such conversation. What follows is the product of that conversation: it is an elaboration and an agreed interpretation of a foster carer's perspective on a major theme of the symposium – the professionalisation of foster care. In addition to the question of financial rewards for foster carers and the implications for the relationship between the carer and the children being looked after, this theme involves the provision of training to foster carers, their assessment and the support they receive. Each of these issues will be addressed in turn.

Love and money in the provision of foster care

The question of whether foster care should be carried out on a voluntary basis for love rather than a fee was a major component of the paper presented by Derek Kirton (Kirton, 2007). Kirton acknowledged the emotional aspect of the dilemma, but rehearsed the tension between these two perspectives by referring predominantly to social theory. Foluke however, on the basis of her experience as a foster carer, illustrated the dilemma by means of psychological theory and the emotional content (sometimes symbolic) of the day-to-day exchanges between the adult carer and the looked after child. Children and young people appear to be acutely sensitive to the terms upon which they are being looked after. Residential workers, for example, may be treated with less respect on the grounds that they are paid to 'take' whatever behaviour they encounter: that is, children refer to the paid status of the workers to legitimise uncooperative or verbally abusive conduct. If foster carers come to be seen as the equivalent to the staff of a residential home, it may be more likely that they will be engaged in such negative exchanges. By way of contrast, a situation was described in which a child who had been looked after appeared to be touched or moved by an act of personal generosity and commitment:

> *Foluke: There was one young person with me and I had to buy him things. He came to me with next to nothing. So I went out and bought trainers, and whatever, and there were a couple of [things bought that were] more than just needs, there were desires [being met] there. And he had gone on a contact [visit] and he came back in and said, 'My dad says that they give you money to get these things'. And I said to him, 'Actually, what they gave me wasn't enough, so I had to spend some of my money'. And I could see him kind of looking at me – in amazement.*

In this example, Foluke's own money which paid for the desired 'extras', might have been not only material, but also symbolic: her willingness to give these tangible resources to the young person demonstrated her 'personal' as opposed to 'professional' commitment.

For Foluke, all of the children and young people who are looked after experience a sense of rejection. Irrespective of the circumstances, they endure a sense of being unwanted or unloved by their family of origin. In consequence, the relationship with the foster carer is crucial: it is a means by which the child can feel appreciated, valued and genuinely cared for. This relationship has the potential to help a child at an emotionally painful time, as well as to facilitate his/her overall development. However, both parties, the child and the foster carer, have to invest in the relationship for it to have significance and benefit. This investment might take many forms, and whilst foster carers should not be driven to financial debt, their unpaid commitment might be an important component – a component that is evident and meaningful to both foster carer and young person. For these reasons Foluke, who said she treated her foster children in the same way as her birth children, was hesitant about, though not against, the current drive towards the professionalisation of foster care.

Training for foster care

For some advocates, the professionalisation of foster care not only involves the provision of fees, but also an extension of the current training for the role (see Kirton, 2007; the Fostering Network, 2008). Foluke acknowledged that in her role of foster carer, she drew on the knowledge base she had gained on her degree course, as well as the knowledge she disseminated as a social work educator. In particular, she made use of attachment and transitions theory (see for example: Atwool, 2006; Golding, 2007; Howe, 2005; Pughe and Philpot, 2007). The insights offered above on the topic of fees appear to be largely informed by attachment theory. The opinion was expressed that these perspectives should be included in the training of all foster carers. However, this raised another question: with the provision of a fee and the requirement to be familiar with this knowledge base, would foster carers be transformed into social workers? At present, children do appear to understand the difference between the two roles. What might be the implications of this blurring?

According to the Fostering Network (2008), the provision of introductory training is ubiquitous, and it is usually their pack *The Skills to Foster* (2003) that forms the foundation of the course. Despite this apparent commitment of local authorities to the principle of training, the on-going provision of events as part of professional development is less in evidence (the Fostering Network, 2008). However, the Independent Fostering Providers (IFPs) have a better reputation in this regard (see Sellick, 2007). Foluke said she had been fortunate in that one of the two local authorities for which she has been registered as a foster carer provided a rolling programme of training opportunities. Although this was appreciated, there was also some criticism: the local authority was said to have been unhelpfully rigid in its approach. This rigidity was particularly manifest in its expectation that all foster carers should participate in the same training events, irrespective of their circumstances and knowledge base. This has meant that, even though Foluke was providing training for foster carers, when she joined a local authority and became a foster carer herself, she was still expected to undertake the introductory course. More recently, even though she has educated social work students on the policy initiative *Every Child Matters* (DfES, 2004), she has been expected to attend a training event on the topic. It was recommended therefore, that local authorities (and possibly IFPs) should abandon the 'one size fits all' approach and individually assess the training needs of foster carers and require participation accordingly. This view has been expressed by other foster carers, and in reflection of this, the principle has been incorporated into the Fostering Network's Policy on training and the professionalisation of foster care (see the Fostering Network, 2008).

Although this charge cannot be made against all local authorities or all training, rigidity can be demonstrated in the way in which courses are delivered. Whilst training packs are of great value, trainers may be inclined to deliver their content uncritically, and give inadequate attention to the possibility that there are times when the content of the course might require adjustment. For example, trainers might use such packs without engaging with the particular strengths or needs of course participants. In consequence, individuals can be treated as categories (trainee foster carers) rather than embodied beings with particular identities and experiences (Clare, 2007). Foluke described the situation in which she was required to sit through the introductory teaching on 'race' and 'racism' without any acknowledgement or recognition of her own identity or experience of being a black woman. However, there was recognition that training is frequently delivered by Family Placement Workers (FPWs) (now known as Supervising Social Workers in some agencies) who have not been specifically educated for the purpose. In consequence, these FPWs may have a poor appreciation of the learning process. Reflexivity was advocated as the means by which trainers might develop their expertise.

The term reflexivity is used in a variety of ways (see D'Cruz et al., 2007). The use of the word here relates to the work of Schön (1983, cited in Pietroni, 1995) in which continuously improved professional practice requires a 'double feedback loop': that is, the professional acts, reflects on the action then both reflects and acts. According to this formula advanced practice requires 'reflection-on-action' as well as 'reflection-in-action'. By means of this approach not only would rigidity and the objectification of course participants be avoided, but the quality of foster carers' learning might be enhanced. Training courses should also facilitate foster carers themselves to engage in reflexive practice. For example, foster carers who have children placed with them might be encouraged to reflect on their day-today methods of relating to children. This particular approach to training and on-going professional development might increase the insight of the foster carers with ultimate benefit for the children in their care.

Assessing and supporting foster carers

The critique of rigidity was also applied to the assessment of foster carers. As with training, standard packs are often used as a means of ensuring that all the essential aspects of an assessment are covered. An over-reliance on the packs exacerbated by an absence of reflexivity can mean that FPWs are insensitive to some of the personal drives to become a foster carer: for example, the complex motivations that involve the anticipation of personal rewards and satisfactions. Instead of engaging with the positive aspects of becoming and being a foster carer, there is a tendency for FPWs to focus on the problems and difficulties that might arise because, according to the dominant content of the pack, the potential foster carer's response to these problems needs to be checked and approved. Whilst this may be important, the assessment can be challenging for participants and not for the 'feint hearted'. The overall conclusion regarding the ability of an applicant may be different however, if positive motivations and strengths are considered as well as the benefits of being a foster carer.

Similarly, the FPW conducting the assessment process can demonstrate an inappropriately rigid adherence to what are considered to be the appropriate values of a foster carer. Although a black woman herself, Foluke felt that the content of the pack that assessed the racial awareness of the potential foster carer was at times unhelpful. For Foluke, human thought and opinion is complex, and the term racist can not be applied without a sophisticated appreciation of the meanings behind a statement of opinion, and the context in which the statement is made. During the course of an assessment some potential foster carers may show a limited understanding of 'race' and fail to convince the FPW of their ability, not only to meet the needs of a black child, but also their ability to inculcate racial respect in the children for whom they care. These people may fail the assessment, not because of their prejudice however, but because they do not have the knowledge and linguistic skills to present themselves in the best light. Such applicants should not be dismissed, but all their strengths and attributes ascertained as well as their limitations. Foluke's perspective is influenced by her own potential to fall foul of the assessment criteria on values: as a practicing Christian she may be (wrongly) perceived to be homophobic. By means of her education however, Foluke can successfully articulate her ability to reconcile Christianity with an appreciation of difference and a respectful approach to diverse sexualities.

The rigidity in the practice of some FPWs may be associated, not only with a lack of reflexivity, but also an absence of independent and critical thought. This weakness in practice is encouraged, not only by assessment packs, but also the content of social work education and agency policies that emphasise a limited notion of 'evidence based practice'. Once research has been undertaken and the subsequent evidence has been marshalled to indicate 'what works', then the government and local agencies use it to develop policies. Students and social work professionals are then encouraged to follow the associated guidance. However, unthinkingly following policy directives or guidance on the basis that it is evidence-led is problematic (Frost, 2002). Frost argues that 'the move towards evidence-led practice tends to oversimplify the complex issues and challenges facing professional social workers in their day-to-day practice' (Frost, 2002, p.39). Although there are a number of problems with evidence-led or evidence based practice, of particular significance here is the idea that general conclusions resulting from research projects can inform what is best or appropriate for specific individuals or families. For example, approving specific applicants to care for children of a certain age only, on the grounds that research suggests this will work best due to the ages of their own birth children, may be too limiting: specific families may have the capability of caring for a broader range of children. In consequence, FPWs need not only to have the ability and experience to appreciate evidence and best practice, but also to assess and make judgements about individual people, their own particular strengths, limitations and circumstances, and whether the best practice guidance will apply.

In relation to the supporting of foster carers, it was noted that the topic was mentioned on numerous occasions throughout the symposium, but the meaning of the term was never elaborated or interrogated. The meaning and practice of support should vary according to the specific needs of foster carers: as with training, 'one size' does not 'fit all'. Given the drive towards the professionalisation of foster care, however, will FPWs become the line managers of foster carers? Will a process of appraisal have to be introduced? If so, this may require FPWs to develop management knowledge and skills. This will demand even more of the workforce just at a time when social work agencies have difficulty in retaining staff (Harlow, 2004). It may be considered an omission, that the crucial role of the FPW was not given attention during the symposium.

Discussion and conclusion

As indicated above, this chapter has been read by Foluke and agreed as an accurate reflection of the conversation, and a fair representation of her experiences and views as a foster carer. However, there is no suggestion that Foluke's views represent the 'truth' of being a foster carer. On the contrary, it is appreciated that the opinions of foster carers will vary in relation to their social characteristics (such as class, gender, 'race' or ethnicity), their personal biographies, but also the context in which their opinions are elicited. Nevertheless, it is useful to examine an important trend, the professionalisation of foster care, from the perspective of someone who has undergone the assessment, training, and day-to-day challenges. Furthermore, comments on the quality of practice in relation to assessment and training may be of value to those responsible for the continued improvement in standards.

From the above it appears as though Foluke is ambivalent about the move towards professionalisation. It might almost be said that Foluke's commitment to treating fostered children as if they were 'her own' belongs to a previous era (Wilson and Evetts, 2006). Despite the arguments as to why the professionalisation of foster care is appropriate (see Kirton, 2007; the Fostering Network, 2008), Foluke is not alone in her ambivalence. This ambivalence is also shared by a number of foster carers, as well as the academics Wilson and Evetts (2006) who argue that the trend does have its problems. In addition to the ambiguities associated with the role as indicated by Foluke, there are ambiguities associated with the term professionalisation. With reference to the relevant literature, Wilson and Evetts (2006) show how professionalisation might mean the development of specialist knowledge and skills, but that it might also mean the promotion of self-interest. Drawing on the work of Fournier (1999), they also argue that the term has been deployed by managers as a disciplinary mechanism: that is, a means by which the practice of workers can be shaped and controlled. Wilson and Evetts have evaluated the deployment of the term professionalisation in relation to foster care and conclude that it is the latter version that is dominant. It is primarily the social service managers in children's departments that are driving the agenda:

The intention is not to give to the workforce the occupational control of the work but rather to regularise and, as far as possible, to standardise it. The control of the work, the selection of the carers, and the determination of what constitutes successful practice and achievement will remain with the social service managers who operate the budgets. This service work will need to be provided within budget and discretion can only be exercised within strict budgetary limits. Similarly, performance by the carers will need to be checked, monitored and constantly demonstrated (Wilson and Evetts, 2006. p.45).

Though tempered by the understanding that there is also a drive to recognise the special skills of foster carers, the conclusion of these academics appears to be negative. Furthermore, the future scenario of regulated and controlled foster care may contrast with the reflexive, independently minded form of practice that is generally preferred by Foluke. Finally, professionalisation of foster care has implications for FPWs in particular and members of the children's workforce as a whole: a matter that will require the continued consideration of bodies such as the General Social Care Council as well as the Children's Workforce Development Council.

References

Atwool, N. (2006) Attachment and resilience: Implications for children in care. *Child Care in Practice*, 12, 4, 315-330

Clare, B. (2007) Promoting deep learning: A teaching, learning and assessment endeavour. *Social Work Education*, 26, 5, 433-446

Department for Education and Skills (DfES) (2004) *Every Child Matters: Change for children*. London: DfES

D'Cruz, H., Gillingham, P., and Melendez, S. (2007) Reflexivity, its meaning and relevance for social work: A critical review of the literature. *British Journal of Social Work*, 37, 1, 73-90

Fournier, V. (1999) The Appeal to 'profesionalisim' as a disciplinary mechanism. *Social Review*, 47, 2, 280-307

Frost, N. (2002) A problematic relationship: Evidence and practice in the workplace. *Social Work & Social Sciences Review*, 10, 1, 38-50

Golding, K. (2007) Attachment theory as a support for foster carers and adoptive parents.*Adoption and Fostering*, 31, 2, 77-79

Harlow, E. (2004) Why don't women want to be social workers anymore? New managerialism, postfeminism, and the shortage of social workers in Social Services Departments in the UK. *European Journal of Social Work*, 7, 2, 167-179

Howe, D. (2005) *Child Abuse and Neglect: Attachment, development and intervention*. Basingstoke: Palgrave Macmillan

Kirton, D. (2007) Step forward? Step back? The professionalisation of fostering. *Social Work and Social Sciences Review*, 13, 1, 6-24

Pietroni, M. (1995) The nature and aims of professional education for social workers: A postmodern perspective. in M. Yelloly and M. Henkel (Eds.) *Learning and Teaching in Social Work. Towards reflective practice*. London: Jessica Kingsley

Pughe, B. and Philpot, T. (2007) *Living Alongside a Child's Recovery: Therapeutic parenting with traumatized children*. London: Jessica Kingsley

Schön, D. (1983) *The Reflective Practitioner*. London: Temple Smith

Sellick, C. (2007) Towards a mixed economy of foster care provision. *Social Work and Social Sciences Review*, 13, 1, 25-40

The Fostering Network (2008) *Towards a Professional Foster Care Service: What it means to be a professional foster carer*. London: the Fostering Network

Wilson, K. and Evetts, J. (2006) The professionalisation of foster care. *Adoption and Fostering*, 30(1), 39-47

7
Kinship care:
What works? Who cares?

Bob Broad

Introduction

This chapter provides an overview of the main research findings on kinship care in the United Kingdom (UK). It identifies key themes emerging from the literature and concludes by making policy and practice recommendations. It is suggested that there is a welcome consensus between researchers and voluntary organisations working in this field about the policy implications arising from the research evidence. The author argues that the publication of such evidence coincides with a new policy opportunity to develop the assessment, identification and funding of services for children living in kinship care. The chapter concludes that whilst kinship care is not a panacea for all neglected or abused children, and that there remain important concerns, these need not prevent this approach being more widely acknowledged for its positive contribution to placement stability, and becoming funded by mainstream monies.

What is kinship care?

In anthropological literature, the term 'kinship care' describes the upbringing of a child by kith and kin, non-blood and blood-related relatives, tribes and friends. In certain cultures, kinship care is the normal way for a child to be brought up and is described in the literature as 'informal kinship care'. By contrast 'formal kinship' care describes an arrangement for a child who has to live away from his or her parental home, is known to the local authority, and is cared for full-time by a member of the child's extended family or a friend. A kinship care placement can be initiated by the local authority, a relative or friend, and involves some sort of assistance or arrangement, including decisions concerning legal orders, financial and social work support. This paper addresses formal kinship care.

The law recognises four different types of formal kinship care in England and Wales. These concern children who are either:

*   fostered with a relative or friend[1];
*   subject to a Residence Order[2];
*   subject to a Special Guardianship Order[3]; or
*   living with family and friends in network support[4].

In England and Wales the *Children Act 1989* is the key legal reference for kinship care as it encourages the placement of a child with a person with whom he/she is familiar: for example, a family member or relative or *'other suitable person'* unless it *'would not be reasonably practicable or consistent with his welfare'*[5]. There is similar legislation covering Scotland (Children (Scotland) Act 1995), Northern Ireland (Children (Northern Ireland) Order) and Ireland (Irish Child Care Act 1991) that is supportive of kinship care.

Kinship care policy

The predominant policy context then, captured in the *Children Act 1989* (S23.6) for England and Wales, is that kinship care is a required first placement consideration for social services and contributes to its search for quality permanent family placements. This context can also be seen to coincide with the re-emergence of both family preservation and resistance to professional permanency solutions for neglected or abused children. More specifically, kinship care contributes to the *Care Matters* (DfES, 2007) and earlier *Quality Protects* initiative (DofH, 1998) on placement stability, by providing another and distinct placement option. Foster care, including relative foster care, has also become the placement of choice with this option accounting for 68% of all children in looked after placements (DfES, 2006a).

In response to unified, determined and research based voluntary sector lobbying of the Department for Education and Skills (DfES), both the Green and White *Care Matters* Papers (DfES, 2006b; DfES, 2007) endorse the principles of kinship care. This appears to be a major breakthrough. Thus, in an apparent welcome change of heart, *Care Matters* acknowledges the importance and contribution of family and friends, stating:

However excellent the range of interventions that is delivered, and however early problems are caught, there will always be cases where children cannot be cared for by their parents alone. Sometimes this means that children will need to enter full-time care. In other cases though it may be possible for care to be shared with other members of the family or with close friends. We believe that this is much better for most children than entering care, and children have told us they believe the same (DfES, 2006b, 2.29).

Yet is *Care Matters* really a breakthrough? It offers no indication of a new statutory, legal, financial and policy kinship care framework. As anticipated by Broad (2006), its endorsement of what it describes as 'family and friends care' centres on practice changes and there is a glaring absence of resource commitments, policy changes or linked up thinking with other government departments, such as housing or the Treasury. For example, in relation to practice, *Care Matters* states that the DfES will:

Require local authorities to lodge with the court at the outset of care proceedings an outline plan for permanence for the child, which they are already required to draw up later in the course of care proceedings. This will provide greater clarity, and at an earlier stage, to all concerned. If a child is not to be supported by family or friends, the plan must make clear why this is not appropriate (DfES, 2006b, 2.30).

The paper then states the government's intention of changing the culture so that the majority of kinship care placements are initiated by family and friends (86% in Farmer and Moyers 2006) and not by social services. The culture should change so that at the outset of care proceedings, local authorities are required to provide an outline permanence plan to the court, including an explanation if a child is not to be supported by family or friends, why this is not appropriate (DfES, 2006b para 2.30).The paper also promises greater promotion of and training on family group conferences. In relation to regulations and guidance, social services providers are already inspected against the *National Minimum Standards Fostering Services Regulations* (DOH, 2002), and these apply to work with all approved foster carers, irrespective of whether they are members of the child's kin.

Numbers of children in kinship care placements

The number of children in kinship care is significant. As at March 31st 2005, 7,500 children (or 12.5% of all 60,900 children 'looked after') were living in family and friends foster placements in England and Wales (DfES, 2006a). These placements have been gradually increasing year-on-year, both as a proportion of all foster placements and as a proportion of all children 'looked after'.

An additional estimated 10%-20% of children categorised as being 'in need' under s.17 *Children Act 1989* also live in kinship care placements. In England, of the 388,200 children 'in need' in 2004 (when the last 'in need' figures were available), an estimated 11,646 children were living in a kinship care arrangement brokered by the local authority, *in addition* to the 7,500 children in family and friends foster placements in the same year.

Kinship care makes an important contribution to placement stability and permanence and its contribution as a placement option is significant. The percentage of children in kinship care placements in England and Wales in March 2005 (12.5% of the total 'looked after' figure) is higher than either the 11% figure for children in children's homes or the 5% figure for children adopted in March 2005. Despite this, the resources dedicated to kinship care and kinship carers are lower[6].

The use of kinship care in Scotland according to Aldgate and McIntosh's research is also increasing, thus:

> Over two thirds (22) of local authorities said they were aware of *an upward trend in the use of kinship care*. Around a fifth of authorities, representing both urban and rural areas, claimed a substantial increase of 50% or more in kinship placements over the last three years, between 2001 and the beginning of 2004. The official returns to the Scottish Executive indicate that the numbers of looked after children in kinship care overall from 2000 to 2003 showed a slight increase. As suggested above, between 2004 and 2005, the national number had risen by 200, endorsing the views of the local authorities gathered half way through the 2004-05 financial year (Scottish Executive 2004 and 2005) (Aldgate and McIntosh 2007, 24, *emphases added*).

UK research messages

The research messages summarised here are based on all the published empirical UK research studies about kinship care (Broad et al, 2001: Broad, 2004; Hunt, 2003, Hunt *et al* 2007; Farmer and Moyers, 2006; Aldgate and McIntosh, 2007). The overall conclusion is that kinship care makes a positive and undervalued contribution to placement stability (*Quality Protects* objective one) and that the majority of children living in such placements would otherwise be looked after by non-relative foster carers. In kinship care, the contribution of committed carers is significant and that of grandparents especially so (Broad et al, 2001; Hunt et al, 2007). However, kinship care is not suitable for all children and the quantifiable improvements in children's lives that result from these arrangements are often at the expense of the carers' health, well being and financial situation. The appeal of kinship care to local authorities is that all or most of the costs of supporting the child are shifted away from the local authority and onto, or in some cases returned to, the child's family. Against the background of a rising demand for permanent placements, a range of kinship care arrangements are contributing to the provision of placement options. It is financially far cheaper for local authorities to make, recommend or broker a kinship care arrangement either under s.17 *Children Act 1989* or under a Residence Order granted by the court under s.8 *Children Act 1989,* than arrange a residential care placement or a family and friends foster care arrangement. This gives rise to a risk that the local authority may resort to potentially unsuitable kinship placements as a way of resolving internal pressures. These include a rise in demand for placements, the lack of placements and pressure on local authority children's services budgets. A further danger arises if kinship placements are not appropriately supported and monitored.

Protective Factors associated with better outcomes

While there are problems associated with kinship arrangements, such as lack of support for the carers, it is also a major contributory factor in providing placement stability (Rowe *et al*, 1989; Jackson and Thomas 1999; Hunt et al, 2007). Kinship care placements appear to offer children greater stability than placements with strangers, although the evidence is not unequivocal on this matter. In relation to the latter, for example, one study found that the proportion of children placed with other family or friends whose placements were continuing at follow-up (59%) was similar to that of those with unrelated foster carers (55%) (Farmer and Moyers, forthcoming). Thus along with greater user (i.e. child) satisfaction, compared with their previous placements, *'contributing to placement stability'* appears to be one of the strongest and recurring themes in the research to date.

Child welfare outcomes for kinship care have been analysed by Hunt et al (2007) in terms of: placement stability; placement quality; relationship quality; child well-being; and overall outcomes. In that study it was found that the following were statistically significant: placement stability; placement with grandparent; previous full time care by index carer; child's acceptance of care; younger children; and no non-sibling children in the household (Hunt et al, 2007). It was found that 72% of kinship care placements were still continuing in 2006 from care proceedings brought by two local authorities between 1995 and 2001, or had ended as long as was needed. Twenty-eight per cent had ended prematurely and 16% were continuing, but vulnerable to disruption. This raises questions about ongoing support and monitoring:

topics that will be addressed later in this paper (Hunt et al, 2007, 1).

Significantly, Hunt et al (2007) found *no* statistical link between any outcome and many other factors tested, viz: child's gender or ethnicity; carer age; which parent the carer was related to; siblings in the placement; other adults in the household; length of social services involvement prior to proceedings; order type; assessment type; whether the child went straight from home to the kinship carer; whether the child was in placement prior to proceedings; and whether concerns were expressed about the placement during proceedings (Hunt et al, 4). Some of these research findings are quite challenging in relation to the assumptions that can be made about the focus of kinship care assessments, as well as their potential complexity.

Profile of kinship carers

Kinship carers have consistently been found to be older, financially disadvantaged, and have more health problems than either the general population or non-relative foster carers. In Farmer and Moyers study (2006, 1) amongst the family and friend carers, grandparents were the largest group (45%) and in Broad's study the figure was 42% (Broad, (2004). In Hunt et al's (2007) study placement with a grandparent was found to be a statistically significant factor in relation to placement stability. Children placed with grandparents were the most likely to remain in the family (86%), followed by those with aunts and uncles (65%) (Farmer and Moyers, 2006). Kin carers are also much more likely than unrelated foster carers to be struggling. For example, 45% kin as opposed to 30% unrelated carers struggled to cope with the children in their care (Farmer and Moyers 2006, 5). As might be expected, family and friends carers showed considerably higher levels of commitment (65% versus 31% in the Farmer and Moyers, forthcoming) to the children they were looking after and a high commitment was related to placement survival. These findings suggest that kin carers are more likely to persevere beyond the point at which unrelated carers concede defeat, even when they are under considerable strain.

Grandparent carers sometimes struggle with feelings of loss and guilt about the difficulties of their adult children which had necessitated the children being removed from them, or because they had been unable to take on a full sibling group. Other grandparents still grieve for the death of the children's parents. In addition, tensions with the children's parents and members of the extended family make caring for the children considerably more difficult (Farmer and Moyers, 2006). We know from other research that a high proportion of grandparents are also in that 'pivotal generation' where they have other inter-generational caring and financial demands placed on them. In consequence, the costs of providing care for their grandchildren can be very high (Broad, 2007).

Family dynamics and child identity

There is evidence that inter- and intra-family relationships are more complicated and stress-prone in kinship care arrangements than in stranger foster care (Sykes et al, 2002). This is because of the family history not found in stranger foster care. There is linked evidence that an understanding of family systems work is vital to understanding inter-generational family dynamics and facilitating effective interventions (Talbot and Calder, 2006). There is also evidence that contact between birth parents, the child and the carer is more likely in a kinship placement than a non-relative placement and that it is often a lively, complex and potentially difficult situation with careful management required (see, for example, Broad, 2006; Geen, 2003). Kinship care also makes a strong contribution to sustaining a child's sense of individual, family identity, and cultural continuity, one of four positive clustered key themes identified by children living in kinship care, another being 'feeling safe in current situation' (Broad, 2006, 16).

Children in kinship care placements

A child's route into kinship care can be 'messy'. In one study (Broad et al, 2001), kinship care was a final resort for social services, the first option by social services, an option chosen by the child following a crisis at home, and finally, where a kinship arrangement was already in place, a continuation of support to the carer. In the same study it was found that 86% of all the children in kinship care placements would otherwise have been removed from home into local authority care, had the arrangement not been made. Most children had already been in local authority care and had negative views of it. In another study it was found that children in relative and non-relative foster care are remarkably similar in terms of their characteristics and the kinds of adversities they had experienced prior to placement (Farmer and Moyers, forthcoming). It is the inconsistent or lack of support to children living in kinship care, who have similar needs to others looked after, which needs to be addressed more consistently.

What do children say about living in kinship care? There is very little evidence on this. However, what there is indicates that children feel loved and supported in ways that do not feature in state care (Broad et al, 2001; Hunt et al, 2007).

Ethnicity

When care is provided by members of the child's birth family, their ethnicity will be shared. In consequence, important considerations concerning the continuity of cultural identity will be attended to. However there is mixed and limited evidence about whether black and minority ethnic families are over-represented in the kinship carers' population. For example, Broad et al (2001) found that there were significantly more black and minority ethnic carers than white kinship carers (whichever the legal order). It was argued that this finding was associated more with the greater number of relatives and friends in the study's black and minority ethnic families than for the white families (Broad et al, 2001). The same study noted that even in a mixed inner London Borough in which the study was undertaken, the proportion of black and minority ethnic families was greater in kinship care than for either the Borough's overall population or its looked after population. However, in another study, although the wider population and ethnicity statistics were not presented, it was found that black and minority ethnic families accounted for a smaller grouping of kinship carers than white carers (Farmer and Moyers forthcoming). Clearly more research is needed on this important policy and practice issue.

Siblings

Although it has been argued that one advantage of family and friends placements is that siblings can be placed together, Broad (2004) found very little evidence of this happening. In Farmer and Moyers study (2006, 1) similar proportions of children were placed with siblings in both relative and non-relative foster care groups (53% versus 52%). In Hunt's research *not* having non-sibling children in the household was a statistically significant factor in placement quality. Thus:

> Only 21% of placements where there were children other than siblings in the household were problem –free compared to 50% of placements where there

were only siblings or the child was placed alone (Hunt *et al*, 2007, 53)

We also know from other research that the presence of a child's siblings in a placement is a major contributory factor to placement stability (Jackson and Thomas 1999). Kinship care offers the opportunity for a child and his/her sibling to be kept and placed together within the same family in a way that other placements do not.

Initiating placements

Although there is some variation between research studies, there is a clear consensus that the overwhelming majority (85% found by Farmer and Moyers, 2006 and 66% by Hunt et al, 2007) are initiated by kin carers rather than social services. The main explanation given for the high 85% figure is that a majority of children (57%) were already in placement when the kinship carer approached social services. An awareness of and work with family and friends networks, family systems and systemic interventions, as well as organisational incentives to do the same, are required for good practice in kinship care to be embedded in local authority practice.

Social services and social work

In the absence of the voluntary sector being systematically involved in providing support services, it is statutory social services personnel who have the key role to play in initiating, finding, assessing and supporting a child and his/her carer. This work is complex and time consuming and for full implementation organisational priority, funding and specialist knowledge is required. No wonder it is patchy. Despite dissatisfaction about the scope, reliability and regularity of services provided, support is welcomed by most children and their carers (Broad et al, 2001). Research has also indicated that there is often confusion within local authorities concerning which type of placement is appropriate for a child being considered for kinship care.

A worrying trend was identified in both Broad's (2001) and Farmer and Moyers' (2006) study of social workers trying to persuade kinship carers to apply for a Residence Order. Such a move would end statutory social work support and weekly foster payments. For some carers the attraction of Residence Orders is that they can help to 'normalise' the family situation.

The critical point here is that if children are at risk of neglect and cared for full time by a carer, then financial and social support should accompany the child, based on the child's needs, and not on the type of legal order.

Some concerns about kinship care

Kinship care is not a panacea -it does not suit every child, and neither does adoption, stranger foster care, Residence Orders or Special Guardianship Orders. As with those other options, kinship care is not 'risk free.' So whilst the research evidence has demonstrated the advantages to many children of living in a kinship care arrangement or placement, there are problems which require acknowledgement.

Kinship care families may be vulnerable to the same sorts of problems faced by other families, including relative poverty, sexual abuse, bullying, violence and substance misuse. Therefore assumptions that family placements are not only best, but always safe are nonsense. For example, there is research evidence that some multiple child abuse involves wider kin networks and there have been non-accidental child deaths in some family placements (Freeman and Ingham, 2006). Additionally, families subject to a kinship care assessment where there is already substance misuse, a large and growing problem within families (Kroll and Cornwall, 2006), are also likely to require a full risk assessment and, if the placement is approved, support packages. If an assessment is borderline abuse/neglect then what levels of support are effective and possible for a network support placement (S.17 Children Act 1989)? There is also a concern that has emerged from the small number of enquiries into deaths of black children in care (for example Tyra Henry) that social services providers have wrongly perceived that child placements within black and minority ethnic families are self-supporting and therefore can be especially trusted, and that minimum support is necessary. Each potential kinship care placement needs an appropriate assessment of risks, resilience and a child and carer support plan.

Finally, in this section, one concern albeit unevidenced, is that the trend towards seeking ever higher numbers of kinship care placements, seen as an untapped resource amidst the ongoing placement crisis will, almost inevitably result in an inappropriate placement being made, resulting either in serious abuse, injury, or death to a child. This is much less likely to happen if the placement is fully assessed, if evidence of parental competence can be independently corroborated, if support services are put in place, and if there is regular placement monitoring. Nevertheless, we know from the research evidence that local authority kinship care policies and practice remain inconsistent, and there is always a risk. Ironically, the policy context to support more children in kinship care placements might increase that level of risk. Kinship care placement numbers are likely to increase if the Department for Education and Skills (DfES) follows the proposal to place a requirement on statutory social services providers to more systematically investigate, and be more accountable for, its kinship care placement decisions (DfES, 2006b, 2.30). In such a climate it is possible that any increase will include both suitable kinship carers, who value being approached early on in placement discussions, as well as kinship carers who are less suitable or willing and who would not have initiated the placement.

The Munby Factor

Articles 8 and 14 of the *European Convention on Human Rights* (*ECHR*) were cited by Justice Munby in his ruling about equitable payments needing to be paid by local authorities to carers based on the needs of the child, and that these should not be affected by the fact that they were placed with members of their own family[7]. This ruling should also effect and potentially 'open up' local authority policies in this area so that there are fewer discrepancies in payments between kinship carers. However, there remains discrimination in some local authorities between the supports, training, and financial assistance received by stranger foster carers compared with relative or friend foster carers (Farmer and Moyers, 2006). Despite the Munby ruling there remain regular legal challenges to local authorities on their service entitlement definitions and practice and these will serve to shape the future direction of kinship care.

Kinship care assessments

Kinship care can be best understood within a local authority's family support and permanency frameworks. A holistic approach needs to be taken of the family involving careful management of the needs of individual members and full assessments. Assessments need to identify a range of appropriate child-centred services, including respite options, and support from the family network for the child and the caregivers (Talbot and Calder, 2006). Specialist kinship care teams and panels make a good contribution to practice for family and friends' foster carers, and other services need to be further identified to meet other kinship carers' needs.

Research has pointed to the highly reactive not proactive stance of local authorities regarding kinship care assessment. In one study, 65% of the kin placements were assessed after the child was already living with the carer (Farmer and Moyers, 2006). There are also concerns about which type of assessment is most suitable as well as concerns about when assessments should be undertaken. Further questions are 'is an assessment always necessary for a member of a child's family or friend?', and 'what type of current assessment framework is appropriate?', 'why isn't there a special assessment framework for kinship carers?' Assessments are complex and can often detract from wider support issues in that the post-assessment support is often lacking. It is especially those carers involved in a network support arrangement (s.17 *Children Act 1989*), and those holding Residence Orders who are especially disadvantaged (see Broad and Skinner, 2005 for a full discussion and examples of different kinship care assessments). It is too soon since Special Guardianship Orders were introduced to assess their contribution.

If a child's welfare is at risk, then the local authority needs to invoke its formal assessment procedures, and potential kinship carers need to be included. This formal assessment should be conducted within the *Fostering Regulations* framework (DOH 2002). It is acknowledged that there is an argument both for changing the assessment procedures for family members being assessed as prospective relative foster carers, as well as for amending the assessment procedures for other kinship care types (Residence Order, Special Guardianship Order and Network Care) where the local authority is also involved. Such an assessment needs to identify risk and resilience areas, and adopt an ecological and family systems approach to its work with families.

Implications for policy and practice

From this review of the research in the UK, most of which has been conducted since 2000, a range of recommendations follow. These are primarily taken from the studies of Aldgate and McIntosh (2007), Hunt *et al* (2007), Farmer and Moyers (forthcoming) and Broad et al (2001), and the Family Rights Group (2007). There is a welcome consensus from these researchers about the future of policy and practice.

There is an unequivocal recommendation that funding and a national framework for organising and supporting kinship care needs to be created. This would ensure that its existing and growing contribution is properly acknowledged, that proper standards are maintained, and it is better supported. In order for this vision to be taken forward, a range of specific policy and practice recommendations inextricably follow:

Policy recommendations

- There needs to be distinct way of assessing potential kinship carers
- Systems need to be put in place for support to be provided to children and kinship carers
- There is a need to introduce a new kinship care financial support framework
- Legal changes are necessary to remove the need for grandparents to seek leave to apply for a Residence Order, in order to gain access to the courts.
- Local authorities need to create specialist kinship care teams and panels and use family placement workers and possibly involve the voluntary sector
- The introduction of a national initiative to encourage and monitor the development of good kinship care policy and practice
- More attention needs to be given to family and friends care in social work education and training
- A new legal category of 'looked after in kinship care' (made in relation to Scotland, see Aldgate and McIntosh 2007)

These policy recommendations are closely aligned with the following practice recommendations:

Practice recommendations

- Local authorities need to have a written policy and set of procedures as well as a leaflet for prospective kinship carers which clearly state what the legal options are, how assessments are made, what the local authority will and will not provide in terms of services, help, advice and financial support
- It is important to acknowledge that a kinship care placement can be of an acceptable standard even if the standard seems to be below that of an approved foster placement.
- More regular monitoring of placements than is currently the case is crucial to ensuring the placement safety and quality
- A consistent, family-owned approach to assessments is needed and should incorporate a holistic family network approach through family group conferencing
- Develop effective care planning in partnership with children and families
- Plan for long-term stability and permanence
- Provide effective social work support
- Other services from health and education are needed

- Social workers need to provide more support to kinship carers and parents
- When there are high levels of conflict with parents or other relatives assistance with contact issues is required
- Help with parenting in order that children's behaviour might be better managed
- Provision of respite care to provide a break for carers who are under strain
- Further financial help for activities for the children
- Access to support groups or peer support

Concluding comments

It is fully recognised that principles of best practice in kinship care are not easy to implement in a child welfare system based on pressurised child protection duties and organisational priorities, and the need for worker and management accountability and risk management. The Department for Children Schools and Families (DCSF) needs to lead on how local authorities can both manage their child protection work and at the same time deliver a wider range of appropriate child placements and family support work. Indeed, research evidence strongly suggests that kinship care should be more fully included in policy and funding frameworks in order to fully support children and carers. All the UK research demonstrates that whilst kinship care has positive outcomes, it also incurs policy and practice complexities in the key areas of providing appropriate support and identifying suitable placements. If statutory social services providers are unable to plan for and fund kinship care, especially 'network support' outside the foster care system (Children Act 1989 S 17) and cope with its demands, it should fund and support the voluntary and independent sector to undertake some of this work, as is the case in New Zealand.

If kinship care is an appropriate, fully assessed and properly supported option, there is evidence that it contributes to positive outcomes for children and is value for money. Ten years ago published research evidence about kinship care in the UK was virtually non-existent (a notable exception was Rowe *et al*, 1989). This was despite the statutory support for the option as set out in the Children Act (1989) (S23. 6). Research conducted over the last ten years and summarised in this article, has confirmed kinship care's contribution and growth.

Up until a few years ago its carer–led origin, and closed marginalised practice, had not generated political interest or professional drive, status or funding such as that afforded to other government led policies (for example, adoption or fostering). This is illustrated by the fact that in excess of twenty DfES staff members have been working on adoption standards, policy, guidance and training for foster care compared with just one person for kinship care. This has now begun to change with a new focus on research, (two studies commissioned by the DfES), a strategic alliance of kinship carers and voluntary organisations, a groundbreaking legal judgement, and a policy acknowledgement in the Green and White *Care Matters* Papers.

Since *Care Matters* was published, the government has declined a suggestion to have a ministerial kinship care task force. Yet there are many other opportunities for policy to be taken forward and for positive changes to be introduced. The voluntary sector's unflagging efforts to engage with the DCSF are very likely to produce some changes although there are no visible signs that the Treasury is discussing financial support for kinship carers. Anticipated guidance and practice amendment will likely result, as in other child protection areas, from a combination of legal judgements, professional and carer group pressures, research findings, policy Initiatives, and ,just possibly, a tragedy. We now know even more about what works in kinship care (research) and we know about how services and support can be provided (best practice). We need to move beyond the rhetoric and see the necessary investment and lead by central government to make kinship care a properly assessed, funded and supported family support and placement option.

Acknowledgements

A special thanks is extended to Joan Hunt (University of Oxford) for granting permission to quote from her study *Keeping them in the family* (Hunt *et al* 2007)

Notes

1. Part III *Children Act 1989* and Regulation 23 *The Fostering Regulations 1991* apply.
2. s.8 *Children Act 1989*.
3. s.115 and Schedule 3 *Adoption and Children Act 2002*, introduced in December 2005.
4. *s.17 Children Act 1989* (child 'in need').
5. s.23 (6) *Children Act 1989.*

6. Munby J 28 September 2001 Manchester judgement *R (on application of L and others) v Manchester City Council* and *R (on application R and another) v Manchester City Council* [2001] EWHC.

7. *R (on application of L and others) v Manchester City Council* and *R (on application R and another) v Manchester City Council* [2001] EWHC

References

Aldgate, J. and McIntosh, M. (2007) *Looking after the Family: A study of children looked after in kinship care in Scotland.* Edinburgh: Social Work Inspection Agency

Broad, B. (2004) Kinship care for children in the UK: Messages from research, lessons for policy and practice. *European Journal of Social Work, 7,* 2, 211-227

Broad, B. (2006) Some advantages and disadvantages of kinship care: A view from research. in M. Talbot and M. Calder, (Eds.) *Assessment in Kinship Care.* Lyme Regis: Russell House (pp.13-24)

Broad, B. (2007) *What is a Grandparent? A digest of key facts.* Harlow: Grandparents Association

Broad, B. (2007) *Kinship care: Providing positive and safe care for children living away from home.* London: Save The Children Fund

Broad, B. and Skinner, A. (2005) *Relative Benefits: Placing children in kinship care.* London: BAAF, London

Broad, B. (Ed.) (2001) *Kinship care: The placement choice for children and young people.* Lyme Regis: Russell House

Broad, B., Hayes, R., and Rushforth, C. (2001 *Kith and Kin: Kinship care for vulnerable young people.* York: Joseph Rowntree Foundation/National Children's Bureau

Department of Health (1998) *Quality Protects.* London: DoH

Department of Health (2002) *Fostering Services National minimum standards, fostering services regulations.* London: DfES

DfES (2006a) *Statistics of Education: Children looked after by local authorities.* Year ending 31 March 2005 Volume 1: Table K. London: DfES

DfES (2006b) *Care Matters: Transforming the lives of children and young people in care.* London: DfES

DfES (2007) *Care Matters: Time for change,* London: DfES

Family Rights Group (2007) *The Role of the State in Supporting Families and Friends Raising Children Who Cannot Live with Their Parents. A policy response to the* Care Matters *Green Paper.* [A joint response from 15 organisations] London: Family Rights Group

Farmer, E. and Moyers, S. (forthcoming) *Kinship Care: Fostering effective family and friends placements.* London: Jessica Kingsley

Farmer, E. and Moyers, S. (2006) *Children placed with family and friends: Placement patterns and outcomes.* executive summary. Bristol: University of Bristol

Freeman, P. and Ingham, J. (2006) Multiple child abuse that involves wider kin networks and family friends within intergenerational networks: A theoretical model. in M. Talbot and M. Calder, (Eds.) *Assessment in Kinship Care.* Lyme Regis: Russell House (pp.87-97)

Geen, R. (2003) The evolution of kinship care policy and practice. *Children, Families and Foster Care* 14, 1, 131-149

Hunt, J. (2003) *Family and Friends Carers.* London: DoH

Hunt, J., Waterhouse, S., and Lutman, E.. (2007) *Keeping Them in the Family: Outcomes for abused and neglected children placed with family and friends carers though care proceedings.* unpublished draft report for DfES. Oxford: University of Oxford

Jackson, S. and Thomas, N. (1999) *What Works in Creating Stability for Looked After Children?* Barkingside, Essex: Barnados

Kroll, B. and Cornwall, J. (2006) The impact of substance misuse on kinship care and the implications for assessment. in M. Talbot and M. Calder, (Eds.) *Assessment in Kinship Care.* Lyme Regis: Russell House (pp.99-121)

Rowe, J., Hundleby, M., and Garnett, L. (1989) *Child Care Now: A survey of placement patterns.* London: BAAF

Scottish Executive (2004) *Statistics Publication Notice. Health and Social Care Series: Children's social work statistics, 2003-4.* available at children@scotland. gsi.gov.uk

Scottish Executive (2005) *Statistics Publication Notice. Health and Social Care Series: Children's social work statistics, 2004-5.* available at children@scotland. gsi.gov.uk

Sykes, J., Sinclair, I., Gibbs, I., and Wilson, K. (2002) Kinship and stranger foster carers: How do they compare? *Adoption and Fostering,* 26, 2, 38-48

Talbot, C. and Calder, M. (Eds.) (2006) *Assessment in Kinship Care.* Lyme Regis: Russell House

8
Lesbian and gay fostering and adoption in the United Kingdom:
Prejudice, progress and the challenges of the present

Janette Logan and Clive Sellick

Introduction

A sea change in law and policy has occurred in the past decade in respect of sexuality and child care in the United Kingdom (UK). At the close of the last Conservative administration, lesbians and gay men were subject to a series of legislative prohibitions. For example, Section 28 of the Local Government Act, 1988 stated that local authorities should not 'promote the teaching in any maintained school of the acceptability of homosexuality as a pretended family relationship.' The discourse enshrined within this legislation functioned as a powerful moral force, with notions of 'pretended family relationships' permeating other aspects of the law (Logan, 2001). The Adoption Act 1976 outlawed the adoption of children by unmarried, including lesbian and gay, couples. Likewise, despite developments in equal opportunities policies, there remained an absence of legislation making discrimination on the grounds of sexual orientation illegal. Much of this has now been swept away. The Adoption and Children Act (2002) finally put an end to the notion of the 'pretend family' (Cosis-Brown and Kershaw, 2008); Section 28 was repealed in 2003; and lesbians and gay men can now become registered as 'civil partners' under the Civil Partnership Act, 2004. Significantly, the fostering and adoption of children by lesbians and gay men is now firmly established in some regions of the United Kingdom (Manchester City Council, 2007; Hicks, 2005a).

Despite all of this, the recent furore surrounding the introduction of the Equality Act (Sexual Orientation) Regulations 2006, is a salutary reminder of the opposition and potential backlash to equality that still exists among some sections of UK. The introduction of the new regulations, aimed at outlawing discrimination against gay people by businesses and service providers, sparked off a furious response from some senior clergy in the Catholic Church and Conservative Party backbenchers. They accused the Government of 'railroading' through gay equality laws that will force Catholic adoption agencies to close (BBC, 2007). A Conservative Member of Parliament, Bill Cash, accused the government of 'giving more preference to those who stand for gay rights than those who are concerned with conscience, with family and with religion' (REF). The head of the Catholic church of England and Wales, Cardinal Cormac Murphy-O'Connor also accused the government of 'an abuse of parliamentary democracy' by rushing through the regulations (BBC, 2007). These responses and those of organisations like the Christian Institute (Christian Institute, 2002a, 2002b) resonate with those levied at the repeal of Section 28 more than five years ago.

In consequence, although there have been positive developments in equality rights generally, and specifically the rights of lesbians and gay men to foster and adopt, the words of Cosis-Brown written in 1992, may still have some relevance:

> social workers and clients live in a world which hates, fears and is fascinated by homosexuality. Social work takes place in this context. (Cosis-Brown, 1992, p.216)

We are now in a position where legislation in the UK, in relation to the protection of some areas of lesbians and gay men's lives, may be more liberal and permissive than 'public opinion' (Cosis-Brown and Kershaw, forthcoming). The insidious nature of the 'corruption' or 'contamination' theory of homosexuality is still held by some and is particularly inflammatory for those working in the child care field and with the young people with whom they work (Logan, 2001). This chapter traces the ideological and legal past that provides the backdrop for the most recent developments in lesbian and gay fostering and adoption. Having established the current context, which offers new opportunities alongside the continuation of prejudice, two important areas for adoptive parents, foster carers and social work practitioners have been identified: firstly, the challenges that might confront gay and lesbian young people and secondly, the process by which gay and lesbian people are assessed by fostering agencies as potential carers. The chapter addresses each of these in turn.

Prejudice and progress

With regards to equal rights for lesbians and gay men, parallels can be drawn from the fight for equal rights for women and racial minorities. However, unlike race and gender, homosexuality has been centrally defined by discourses of morality (Warner, 1993). Social conservatives draw upon a set of beliefs, ideological positions and institutional practices that have been sanctioned by religion, medicine, law and culture and which specify the nature of heterosexual superiority and homosexual inferiority (Fish, 2007). Homosexuals have been viewed as inherently threatening to institutional heterosexuality, to children, to family life and to morality. Such perspectives are evident in legislation which historically has constructed homosexuals as criminals, deviants and mentally ill. Even when homosexuality was decriminalised by the 1967 Sexual Offences Act, homosexuality was still regulated and confined to the private domain. As indicated above, section 28 blatantly determined that same sex families were inferior as they were *pretended* family relationships rather than real ones (Fish, 2007).

In addition, lesbians and gay men have long been denied the opportunity to enjoy a family unit that involves children. They have often lost custody cases, been denied access to fertility services and been barred from jointly adopting children.

This ideology of heterosexism has been acutely borne out in the debate about the rights of lesbians and gay men to foster children. The privileged (and taken for granted) status of heterosexuality means that it is seen as natural, normative, morally neutral and ideal and is therefore the preferred living arrangement in which to bring up children. In contrast, fears abound that if children were to be raised by same sex couples it would be detrimental to their development, they would be subject to sexual abuse and bullying, or would grow up lesbian or gay themselves.

The 1976 Adoption Act allowed the adoption of children by single people and by the late 1980s a few lesbians and gay men had been successful in their applications to become foster or adoptive parents. However, many had not been open about their sexuality fearing it would jeopardise their chances of approval, so the practice remained hidden (Logan, 2001; Hicks, 2005a). In 1988, Skeates and Jabri published the first UK report on fostering and adoption by lesbians and gay men. They argued that opposition to lesbian and gay foster care and adoption was founded on stereotypical and discriminatory assumptions. When lesbian and gay applicants were open about their sexuality they did not receive positive responses from agencies. Further research carried out in the early 1990s highlighted that when lesbians and gay men were approved as carers they either did not have children placed with them or were expected to take disabled children or to provide only short term fostering or respite care (Hicks, 1996). In contrast, when social workers were able to speak on the subject, they indicated that lesbian and gay carers made valuable contributions to serving the best interests of children (Skeates and Jabri, 1988). However, this, and evidence that children raised by lesbian or gay carers are no more disadvantaged than those raised by heterosexuals, (Tasker and Golombok, 1991; Golombok, 2000) was conveniently ignored. A consultation paper on family placement published by the former Government in 1990 under the Children Act, 1989 specifically addressed sexuality in relation to foster care:

> It would be wrong to arbitrarily exclude any particular groups of people from consideration. But the chosen way of life of some adults may mean that they would not be able to provide a suitable environment for the care and nurture of a child. No one has the 'right' to be a foster parent. 'Equal rights' and 'gay rights' policies have no place in fostering services (Department of Health, 1990, para 16)

The 'gay rights' phrase provoked much protest from many individuals and child care organisations and was subsequently removed. However, the scope for discrimination remained against lesbians and gay men whose '*chosen* way of life' may have been considered inappropriate for foster care. The White Paper on Adoption (Department of Health, 1993) reaffirmed the Government's position that the adoption of children should be the prerogative of heterosexuals (preferably married couples). Although lesbians and gay men could apply to adopt as single applicants, many local authorities remained reluctant to approve or use (known) lesbian or gay carers for fear of the widespread public and media criticism that this may have evoked (Hicks and McDermott, 1999). Since the late 1980s and early 1990s there has been what Hicks has termed a 'quiet revolution' whereby lesbians and gay men have 'pushed against social, legal and state practices to achieve their desires to foster or adopt children' (Hicks, 2006, p.763). For a detailed analysis of the trajectory of this debate and subsequent developments, see Hicks (2005a).

Eventually, in 2002, after prolonged debate, the Adoption and Children Act was introduced, replacing the Adoption Act 1976 to bring adoption law in line with the Children Act 1989. For the first time, unmarried couples, including lesbians and gay men, were allowed to adopt jointly. Not surprisingly, there was considerable opposition to the inclusion of lesbian and gay couples. Arguments were made that married heterosexual couples are always best for children and that adoption by same sex couples should be outlawed, used only as a last resort or in particular circumstances, demonstrating that the prejudice of the past has continued (Hicks, 2005a). Baroness O'Cathain, speaking for the Conservative Party during the parliamentary debate on the Adoption and Children Bill in the House of Lords, clearly asserted the view that lesbian and gay families are a threat to society and family values:

By extending the category of would be adopters to include homosexual couples of both genders and cohabiting heterosexuals, I contend that the Bill is now being used as an instrument of social engineering.... Is it political correctness? Is it social engineering? Or – perish the thought – is it the permanent downgrading of marriage and the family? I repeat that it is the children that I am concerned about. (House of Lords debate on Adoption and Children Bill, 16 October 2002, column 882-3, cited in Hicks, 2005b)

The Christian Institute was particularly active in opposing this legislation and funded publications which they distributed to every adoption panel in the UK, arguing that to place children with lesbian or gay carers would mean they would suffer stigma and/or psychological or sexual damage (Christian Institute, 2002a). Morgan (2002) went on to claim that 'homosexual adoption is now unquestioned in social work orthodoxy' (Morgan, 2002, p.9). In response, Hicks notes that

whilst most of these claims lack substance and are easily disputed, 'their arguments cannot be so easily dismissed as they draw upon and reinforce homophobic ideas about gay parenting held by many, including some social work professionals' (Hicks, 2005a, p.51).

Whilst much of the debate has, in the main, focussed on adoption, the same questions and issues are relevant to foster care within a wider context of prejudice.The Fostering Services Regulations and National Minimum Standards (Department of Health, 2002) for foster care value equality and diversity whilst the recent Green Paper, *Care Matters* (DfES, 2006) reiterates this position.

The challenges facing lesbian and gay young people

In general, the debate on lesbian and gay fostering and adoption has focussed on the rights or otherwise of adults to become carers and parents. However, it is also important to consider lesbian and gay young people as little attention has been given to their particular needs (Mercer and Berger, 1989). Social workers and foster carers may find themselves working with young people in the 'looked after' system who identify as lesbian or gay. These young people may be struggling to come to terms with their sexuality. Adolescence can be a difficult time for any young person, irrespective of their sexual orientation, yet lesbian and gay young people have to negotiate peer group pressure and gender stereotyping within the context of feeling different. In addition, young people in the 'looked after' system will be troubled in other ways and may be coming to terms with loss and separation from their family. For some young people, their sexual orientation and its consequences may be the reason for their separation (Logan, 2001).

The discrimination, social stigma, and prejudice attached to being a young gay male or lesbian can have a profound impact on psychological adjustment and well-being. As a consequence they are a 'high risk' population for social, psychological and health concerns (Hippler, 1986), and are at increased risk of drug abuse, depression, suicide, pregnancy and HIV infection (Gibson, 1989; Remafedi et al., 1991). Findings from a recent survey into homophobic bullying in schools (Stonewall, 2007) are a chilling reminder of the deeply entrenched stigma and prejudice to which young lesbians and gay men are subject. *The School Report,* the largest poll of its kind ever conducted in Great Britain, reported that homophobic bullying was extensive in Britain's schools (Stonewall, 2007). It found that 65% of lesbian and gay pupils had experienced homophobic bullying, including verbal and physical bullying and death threats. Alarmingly, 30% of lesbian and gay pupils said that adults (including teachers or support staff) were responsible for homophobic incidents in their schools and half of teachers failed to respond to homophobic language when they heard it.

Given this context, it is hardly surprising that the process of developing a positive sexual identity can be long and complex and whilst some young people may acknowledge feeling different many do not 'come out' until their early 20s (Savin-Williams and Rodriguez, 1993). 'Coming out' can be one of the most difficult and potentially traumatic experiences a gay person undertakes (Moses and Hawkins, 1982) and is vividly illustrated by the words of one young person:

> Why can't we say why we are hurting? I was desperate. I wanted to tell you how much I needed your help but I couldn't. I was convinced that the only way I could be accepted was to remain hidden. I was sure that no-one would love me if they knew. I was desperate. I couldn't continue. I withdrew from school and almost killed myself. (Baker, 1985).

Despite being a 'high risk' population, the needs and experiences of lesbian and gay young people remain either ignored or unmet (Logan, 2001). A number of authors have argued, in relation to lesbian and gay youth, that social workers and other personnel are ill informed or even discriminatory, that agencies lack relevant policies, and that lesbian and gay youth face silencing and denial of their sexual orientation (Saperstein, 1981; Vergara, 1984; Hunter and Schaecher, 1987; Mallon, 1992; Sullivan, 1994). Some caution needs to be exercised here as these arguments were made in an earlier period and in a different country. However, professional intervention may be improved if some of the fundamental recommendations made by Mercer and Berger (1989) are followed. These include: continuing education and training on the topic of lesbian and gay identity formation; challenging homophobia; and making appropriate referrals for adolescents who identify themselves as lesbian or gay. More recently O'Brien (1999) in her research into social work practice with lesbian and gay young people, concluded that 'heteronormativity' is continually constructed and homosexuality pathologized within everyday practices of social work.

Unlike in the USA the needs of young people and their sexual identity have been acknowledged in law in the UK through the Children Act, 1989 and its accompanying standards and guidance. This includes for example the statement that:

> The needs and concerns of young gay men and women must ... be recognised and approached sympathetically (DoH, 1991, p.97).

and that

> Gay men and women may require very sympathetic carers to enable them to accept their sexuality and develop their own self esteem (DoH, 1991, p.98)

The Fostering Services National Minimum Standards (Department of Health, 2002) reiterates that foster care services should meet the needs of lesbian and gay young people by stating that fostering agencies had to ensure that:

> ...each child and his/her family have access to foster care services which recognise and address her/his needs in terms of gender, religion, ethnic origin, language, culture, disability and sexuality. (Department of Health, 2002, p.11)

The process of accepting, understanding and promoting the human rights of lesbian and gay young people has reflected changing mindsets more broadly with regard to lesbians and gay adults. However, there are also hostile voices towards both young people and adults who are gay and these have been given expression through harassment and violence. One placment agency, the Albert Kennedy Trust, was established following the death of a 16 year old child who had run away from a local authority children's home in 1989 and who died whilst trying to escape from a gang of homophobic bullies. The Trust provides foster placements to young lesbians and gay men (Albert Kennedy Trust, 2008) and a service consistent with the relevant Regulations and Minimum Standards (Department of Health, 2002). As in other areas of child welfare, this is an example of the independent sector pioneering innovative services which the public sector may implement more widely (Sellick and Howell, 2004; Manchester City Council, 2007).

The process of assessment:
The experiences of lesbian and gay applicants

Since fostering and adoption by same sex couples gained legal and policy legitimacy, the debate has moved on and different issues are now being raised. The current Government's stance is clearly one of 'no discrimination'. Some commentators claim that this position underestimates the complexity of social work practice particularly in the assessment and support of lesbian and gay foster carers and adopters (Hicks, 2000, 2005a). The issues raised earlier in this paper indicate that changes in the law are not alone sufficient to change general attitudes. Within a wider context of prejudice and stereotypes, social workers may be left not knowing *how* to work with lesbian and gay applicants. The debate has shifted from whether or not lesbians and gay men are suitable as carers, to a more critical examination of the *process* of their becoming approved, and the extent to which social work practice continues to reinforce and perpetuate the superiority of heterosexuality. Research into the experiences of prospective lesbian and gay carers highlights the 'heteronormativity' underlying social work practice, a practice which continues to uphold the 'gold standard' of married heterosexual carers, and which, at best, accepts that lesbians and gay men can appropriately foster or adopt so long as they prove themselves to be no different to heterosexual carers, but at worst, perpetuates the notion that lesbian and gay carers are second best or a last resort (Hicks, 2005b and 2005c).

Early research into the experiences of lesbian and gay applicants has shown that they were often subjected to more scrutiny than heterosexual applicants (Hicks, 1996; Ricketts and Achtenberg, 1990). Social workers often knew very little about lesbian or gay lives and either failed to address sexuality at all or focussed on it to the extreme (Hicks, 1996; Cosis-Brown, 1998). Evidence from both social workers and lesbian and gay carers and applicants suggest that 'normalising' strategies were being used in the assessment process, particularly in relation to gender concerns. So social work home studies explored how applicants would provide appropriate gender role models, if they knew members of the opposite sex and whether they would ensure that their children came into contact with a range of both men and women. In Hicks' view, the pre-occupation with problematic gender roles or social development is actually about maintaining and promoting traditional views of both the family and roles of men and women (Hicks, 2000).

Recent publications which explored the roles and perceptions of male foster carers (Newstone, 2000; Wrighton, 2006; Wilson *et al*, 2007) suggest that a traditional view of gender tasks endures amongst foster carers themselves. For example Wilson and her colleagues found that men chose to deal with 'masculine' issues such as contact with the police (Wilson et al., 2007). A male foster carer in Newstone's exploration of men as role models commented that 'men are different from women and need to provide a role model that gives a child a balanced view of society' (Newstone, 2000, p.37). This may seem a dated and disputed view but it is clear that many fostered children and young people have been maltreated by men in a position of trust. Male foster carers, including those who are gay, are well-placed to compensate both for the harm experienced by children and the distorted image of men as carers. As Sellick and Connolly noted in their national survey of independent fostering agencies 'male foster carers can provide positive and compensatory care to children whose experiences of men has been distorted by harmful events' (Sellick and Connolly, 2002, p.113).

Even when practitioners are supportive, open-minded and able to think beyond traditional boundaries, there is still much confusion about *how* to assess lesbian and gay applicants, and social workers struggling with assessments are a feature of all related research (Hicks and McDermott, 1999; Brooks and Goldberg, 2001; Ryan, 2000; Ryan *et al*, 2004). In these studies social workers were unclear about how to talk about sexuality. Should they ask different questions of lesbian and gay applicants when an 'equality' stance usually means asking the same of everyone? Hicks argues there is a need to move on from 'sameness' models, which suggest that lesbian and gay carers are 'just like' heterosexuals, towards acknowledging the different experiences that being a lesbian or gay carer may bring (Hicks, 2005a). Central to the assessment of lesbian and gay applicants are explorations of their experiences of adolescence, how their sexuality has impacted on their lives and family relationships, and how they deal with prejudice and discrimination. Questions related to these issues *do* need asking, albeit in a holistic sense and in the context of caring for some one else's child. Hicks (2005a) hopes that as lesbian and gay carers gain more experience, they will feel less need to argue they are simply 'just as good as heterosexual carers' and instead can point to their differences, thereby promoting new ideas about family and kinship practices.

Recent research in the USA supports this position (Goldberg et al., 2007). In a study of 35 lesbian couples seeking to adopt, three key areas related to agency and worker inclusion and acceptance were identified. Firstly, lesbian applicants noted having their relationships validated and valued and of being 'respected and welcomed as same sex couples' (p.56). Secondly, they appreciated evidence of positive attitudes towards the gay community through, for example, the publication of images of same-sex couples in recruitment material on agency websites. Thirdly, these lesbian applicants valued the professional nature of the agency. They particularly appreciated their assessment and the support they received in 'explicitly preparing them for the challenges that they would face adopting as a couple' (p.57).

Conclusion

Despite the historical and on-going context of prejudice, the policy agenda has shifted significantly, particularly over the past decade. There is now a legislative framework in place which protects and promotes the interests of lesbian and gay young people and lesbian and gay adults wishing to foster or adopt. We have come a long way since the early 1980s when lesbian and gay fostering and adoption was largely unheard of and sexuality not even broached on general social work education courses. Whilst opposing voices and forces remain, the current Government's 'non-discriminatory' stance means that lesbian and gay fostering and adoption is well established in some regions of the UK. As this chapter has indicated however, legislative and policy change does not remove the challenges for social workers. These challenges include, offering sensitive and appropriate support to gay and lesbian young people who are 'looked after', as well as assessing gay men and lesbians who apply to become foster carers. Within this complex social context, many social workers, foster carers, parents and young people believe that real progress has been achieved in the world of adoption and fostering.

References

Albert Kennedy Trust (2008) www.akt.org.uk/ accessed 14th May 2008

Baker, D. (1985) Beyond rejection: The church, homosexuality and hope, cited in T. Gullotta, G. Adams and R. Montemayor (Eds.) (1993) *Adolescent Sexuality.* London: Sage

BBC News (2007) 21st March, 2007. http.//news.bbc.co.uk/1/hi/education/6239098.stm

Brooks, D. and Goldberg, S. (2001) Gay and Lesbian Adoptive and Foster Care Placements: Can they meet the needs of waiting children? *Adoption and Fostering*, 15, 2, 11-17

Christian Institute (2002a) *Adoption Law: Sidelining stability and security,* Newcastle-upon-Tyne: Christian Institute. www.christian.org.uk/html-publications/adoption_briefing2.htm

Christian Institute (2002b) *Same-Sex Parenting is Bad for Kids.* Newcastle-upon-Tyne, Christian Institute; www.christian.org.uk/pressreleases/2002/february_06_2002/htm check URL

Cosis-Brown, H. (1992) Lesbians, the state and social work practice: M. Langan and L. Day (Eds.) *Women, Oppression and Social Work.* London: Routledge

Cosis-Brown, H. (1998) *Social Work and Sexuality: Working with lesbians and gay men. Basingstoke:* Palgrave Macmillan

Cosis-Brown, H. and Kershaw, S. (2008) The legal context for social work with lesbians and gay men: Updating the educational context. *Social Work Education, 27,2,122-130*

Department of Health (1990) *Foster Placement (Guidance and Regulations).* Consultation Paper No. 16. London: HMSO

Department of Health (1991) *The Children Act 1989, Guidance and Regulations, Volume 3: Family placements.* London: HMSO

Department of Health, Welsh Office, Home office and Lord Chancellors' Department, *Adoption: The future.,* London:HMSO

Department of Health (2002) *Fostering Services National Minimum Standards and Fostering Services Regulations.* London: The Stationary Office

Department for Education and Skills (2006) *Care Matters: Transforming the lives of children and young people in care.* Norwich: The Stationary Office

Fish, J. (2007) *Heterosexism in Health and Social Care.* London: Palgrave MacMillan

Gibson, P., (1989) *Gay Male and Lesbian Youth Suicide.* cited in R.C. Savin-Williams and R.G. Rodriguez (1993) Lesbian, gay and bisexual youths. in T. Gullotta, G Adams, and R. Montemayor (Eds.) *Adolescent Sexuality.* London: Sage

Goldberg, A., Downing, J., and Sauck, C. (2007) Choices, challenges and tensions: Perspectives of lesbian prospective adoptive parents. *Adoption Quarterly,* 10, 2, 33-64

Golombok, S. (2000) *Parenting: What really counts?* London: Routledge

Hicks, S. (1996) The 'last resort'? Lesbian and gay experiences of the social work assessment process in fostering and adoption. *Practice,* 8, 2, 15-24

Hicks, S. (2000) Good lesbian, bad lesbian. Regulating heterosexuality in fostering and adoption assessments.. *Child and Family Social Work,* 5, 2, 157-168

Hicks, S. (2005a) Lesbian and gay foster care and adoption. A brief UK history. *Adoption and Fostering,* 29, 3, 42-56

Hicks, S. (2005b) Queer genealogies: Tales of conformity and rebellion amongst lesbian and gay foster carers and adopters. *Qualitative Social Work,* 4, 3 93-308

Hicks, S. (2005c) Is gay parenting bad for kids? Responding to the 'very idea of difference' in research on lesbian and gay parents. *Sexualities,* 8, 2, 153-168

Hicks, S. (2006) Genealogy's Desire; Practices of kinship amongst lesbian and gay foster carers and adopters. *British Journal of Social Work,* 36, 761-776

Hicks, S. and McDermott, J. (Eds.) (1999) *Lesbian and Gay Fostering and Adoption: Extraordinary yet ordinary.* London: Jessica Kingsley

Hippler, M. (1986) The problems and promise of gay youth. *Advocate, p.42*

Hunter, J. and Schaecher, R. (1987) Stresses on lesbian and gay adolescents in schools. *Social Work in Education,* 9, 3, 180-90

Logan, J. (2001) Sexuality, child care and social work education. *Social Work Education,* 20, 5, 563-575

Mallon, G. (1992) Gay and no place to go: Assessing the needs of gay and lesbian adolescents in out of home settings. *Child Welfare,* 71, 6, 547-56

Manchester City Council, Children, Families and Social Care (2007) *Practice Guidance on Assessing Gay and Lesbian Foster Care and Adoption Applicants.*

Manchester: Manchester City Council

Mercer, L.R. and Berger, R.M. (1989) Social service needs of lesbian and gay adolescents: Telling it their way. in P. Allen-Meares and C. Hoenk Schapiro (Eds.) *Adolescent Sexuality: New challenges for social workers.* Binghampton, NY: Haworth

Morgan, P. (2002) *Children as Trophies? Examining the evidence on same sex parenting.* Newcastle-upon-Tyne: Christian Institute

Moses, E.A. and Hawkins, R.O., (1982) *Counselling Lesbian Women and Gay Men: A life issues approach.* St Louis, MO: C.V. Mosby

Newstone, S. (2000) Male foster carers: What do we mean by 'role models'? *Adoption and Fostering,* 24, 3, 36-47

O'Brien, C.A. (1999) Contested territory: Sexualities and social work. in A.S. Chambon, A. Irving, and L. Epstein (Eds.) *Reading Foucault for Social Work.* New York: Columbia University Press

Remafedi, G., Farrow, J.A., and Deisher, R.W. (1991) Risk factors for attempted suicide in gay and bisexual youth. *Paediatrics,* 87, 869-875

Ricketts, W. and Achtenberg, R. (1990) Adoption and foster parenting for lesbians and gay men: Ccreating new traditions in family. *Marriage and Family Review,* 14, 3/4, 83-118

Ryan, S.D. (2000) Examining social workers' placement recommendations of children with gay and lesbian adoptive parents. *Families in Society: The journal of contemporary human services,* 81, 5, 517-528

Ryan, S.D., Pearlmutter, S., and Groza, V. (2004) Coming out of the closet: Opening agencies to gay and lesbian adoptive parents. *Social Work,* 49, 910, 85-95

Saperstein, S. (1981) Lesbian and gay adolescents: The need for family support. *Catalyst,* 3, 4, 61-70

Savin-Williams, R. and Rodriquez, R. (1993) Lesbian, gay and bisexual youths. in T. Gullotta, G. Adams, and R. Montemayor (Eds.) *Adolescent Sexuality.* London: Sage

Sellick, C. and Connolly, J. (2002) Independent fostering agencies uncovered: the findings of a national study. *Child and Family Social Work,* 7, 2, 107-120

Sellick, C. and Howell, D. (2004) A description and analysis of multi-sectoral fostering in the United Kingdom. *British Journal of Social Work,* 34, 4, 481-499

Skeates, J. and Jabri, D. (Eds.) (1988) *Fostering and Adoption by Lesbians and Gay Men.* London: London Strategic Policy Unit

Stonewall (2007) *The School Report.* www.stonewall.org.uk/media/current_releases/1793.asp

Sullivan, T.R. (1994) Obstacles to effective child welfare service with gay and lesbian youths. *Child Welfare,* 73, 4, 291-304

Tasker, F. and Golombok, S. (1991) Children raised by lesbian mothers: The empirical evidence. *Family law,* 21, 184-187

Vergara, T.L. (1984) Meeting the needs of sexual minority youth: One programmes response. in Schoenburg, R.. and Goldberg, R.S. (Eds.) *Homosexuality and*

Social Work. Binghampton, NY: Haworth

Warner, M. (1993) *Fear of a Queer Planet: Queer politics and social theory.* Minneapolis: University of Minnesota Press

Wilson, K., Fyson, R., and Newstone, S. (2007) Foster fathers: Their experiences and contributions to fostering. *Child and Family Social Work,* 12, 1, 22-31

Wrighton, P. / British Association for Fostering and Adoption (2006) *The Role of Male Carers in Adoption and Fostering.* Practice Note, 49. London: BAAF

9
What matters in fostering adolescents?

Jo Lipscombe and Elaine Farmer

Introduction

Over recent years the proportion of adolescents looked after by foster carers has increased (Sinclair et al., 1995; Triseliotis et al, 1995; Packman and Hall, 1998; Department for Education and Skills (DfES), 2006) and it is known that the disruption rate for these placements is high (Triseliotis et al., 1995; Thoburn et al., 2000; Farmer et al, 2004; Sinclair et al, 2004a). The Green Paper *Care Matters: Transforming the lives of children and young people in care* (DfES, 2006) and the subsequent White Paper *Care Matters: Time for change* (DfES 2007) discuss the development of Multidimensional Treatment Foster Care (MTFC) for adolescents with extremely challenging behaviour and the wider extension of aspects of this programme. A tiered system of placement types for all other children, based upon the individual needs and requirements of the child, will be used to inform commissioning. However, neither paper attempted to delineate the specific task of fostering teenagers as opposed to younger children, even though the fostering of adolescents entails a range of issues and care-taking tasks specific to this age group that are less or not relevant to younger children. Whilst some adolescents will need the high level of support offered by MTFC and the Youth Justice Board (YJB) equivalent, Intensive Fostering, many adolescents will be well served by skilled foster carers with experience and knowledge of their needs. Given the challenges of caring for fostered adolescents (Walker et al., 2002; Farmer et al., 2004; Sinclair et al., 2004a), it is essential that appropriate training and support is provided for the carers of adolescents and the social workers supporting these placements, an issue that has gained recognition in the White Paper.

Adolescence is, in itself, a period of considerable ambiguity, which typically involves delicate negotiations between young people and their parents (Jones and Wallace, 1992). For looked after adolescents, this time can be even more challenging. For example, while young people living with their birth families are generally planning future occupations and qualifications, the priorities for adolescents in the care system may be in dealing with their relationships with family members or preparing to cope with early independence (Ward, 1995; Farmer and Moyers, forthcoming). Young people in care have to make a secure base in the foster family at the same time as they are striving to establish their autonomy. Similarly, they need to form their own identity while separated from their birth families (Aldgate et al., 1989). However, as a result of previous experiences and the number of adversities in their background histories, some adolescents in the care system are not yet ready for these developmental tasks. Conflicting loyalties and ambivalent feelings towards members of their birth families may further complicate this stage for some looked after teenagers. Downes (1992) concluded that foster families should provide fostered adolescents with a secure base from which they can reappraise and re-negotiate significant relationships, gain confidence in the wider world, and develop the capacity for mature independence.

Although there are plans in the White Paper for looked after children to remain in care until they are 21 (and a presumption that they will remain at least until they are 18), the average age of leaving home for non-looked-after children is 24 (A National Voice, 2005). Further, the foster care system depends upon turnover to function, with children being 'exported' either to home or independent living (Sinclair, 2005). Given the current shortage of foster placements and the difficulties in recruiting sufficient carers, it will be a real challenge for local authorities to balance the tensions between providing foster placements for new care entrants and allowing existing looked after children to remain in their placements for longer. Thus, while the situation for care leavers is improving, they are still expected to be independent at an earlier age than their non-looked after peers, and there is a heightened need for them to attain tangible life skills whilst in placement to enable them to deal confidently with the transition to adulthood.

It is possible that policy and practice initiatives on fostering adolescents will become either overshadowed by developments such as MTFC and Intensive Fostering, or subsumed within general fostering for all children. We would therefore argue that care needs to be taken to ensure that the skills necessary for working with adolescents are recognised. The research on which this paper is based identified a series of particular parenting skills and supports that contributed to successful outcomes for fostered adolescents, which will be discussed below, once the research study has been outlined.

The research

The research was funded by the Department of Health (Farmer et al., 2004) and was conducted in England. The primary aim was to discover how far foster carers' parenting strategies and the supports they receive relate to the outcomes of placements for adolescents, and which other characteristics within the child or the foster family relate to the stability and effectiveness of placements.

The study used a one year prospective, repeated measures design and was based on a consecutive sample of 68 newly placed young people aged 11 to 17, whose reasons for admission included concerns about their current behaviour and/or emotional well-being. The young people were drawn from specialist and mainstream fostering schemes in 14 local authorities and two independent fostering agencies. Certain types of placement and categories of young people were excluded as the caring skills necessary in these situations, or the supports provided, were considered likely to be markedly different from the target population. Therefore young people in respite placements, mother and baby placements, those remanded to foster care, young people with severe learning difficulties. and asylum seekers were not included. Placements with family or friends were also not included as these formed the basis for a separate study of kinship care (Farmer and Moyers, forthcoming).

Data were collected in three ways: through a review of the young people's case files; through semi-structured interviews with the young people, their foster carers and social workers; and by standardised measures. Interviews were conducted at three months and 12 months after the start of the placement, or at the point of ending if this occurred earlier. Two outcome measures were chosen to provide a broad overview of the placement:

1. a simple rating of placement disruption or continuation (40% of the placements had disrupted by the 12 month follow-up);
2. a rating of the quality (or 'success') of the placement for the young people, in terms of how beneficial the placement had been for them.

Forty seven per cent of the placements were rated as 'successful' because they were continuing well or had had planned positive endings by the one year follow-up.

The foster carers

Just under a third of the foster carers were single (31%), while the remainder had a partner. The ages of the carers ranged from 28 to 67 years, with just over half (53%) aged between 41 and 50 years old. Ninety three per cent of the carers were white and of British origin; one was from a European background, two were African-Caribbean and two were of mixed ethnicity. Four per cent of the carers had been fostering for less than a year and 33% for between one and five years. Nearly a quarter (24%) had been fostering for between five and 10 years, 21% for 10-15 years and a further 18% for 15 years or more. Moreover, 62% of the carers were part of a specialist fostering scheme.

The young people

Of the 68 young people interviewed, 35 (51%) were girls and 33 (49%) were boys. Their ages ranged from 11 to 17, with a mean age of 14.25 years. Eighteen per cent of the young people were from black or minority ethnic backgrounds, including nine young people who were of mixed ethnicity, two who were African-Caribbean and one who was Asian. Eighty three per cent of the young people were placed with foster carers of the same ethnic origin. As would be expected, analysis of the young people's case files indicated that the majority of the young people had experienced marked adversities during their childhood, including family disruption, physical and sexual abuse and neglect.

Not surprisingly, given the extent of these adversities, the young people in the sample often had complex care histories; only 39% of the young people had no previous experience of care, although some of these had been looked after by family or friends. The young people also demonstrated many behavioural and emotional difficulties. For example, over two thirds showed challenging behaviour at home (76%) or outside the home (68%), and over half (56%) displayed violent or aggressive behaviour. Forty per cent had either been cautioned or had a criminal conviction, and 32% had abused drugs or alcohol. Almost a fifth (18%) were involved in risky sexual relationships and 16% showed inappropriate sexual behaviour, with a further seven per cent showing sexually abusing behaviour. Just over a fifth (22%) had self-harmed and 12% had attempted suicide. Furthermore, many of the young people had a disrupted educational history.

Parenting fostered adolescents

As outlined above, the previous experiences of looked after adolescents and the number of adversities they have suffered, combined with their age, mean that there are a number of specific care-taking or 'parenting' issues that need to be addressed within placements that are less relevant or which play out differently with younger fostered children. These issues include being able to respond sensitively to the young people, including responding to the young person's emotional age as well as their chronological age, facilitating their education and peer relationships, promoting their sexual health and relationships, and balancing the young person's need for safety with that for autonomy, in preparation for independent living. Carers also need to work with social workers to manage the young person's contact with their birth family, as will be discussed in detail later.

Sensitive responding

Talking about the past and about family relationships

Many young people in care may need to talk about their past histories and birth family relationships with an adult whom they trust. We found that placements were less likely to disrupt when the foster carers had been receptive to the young person's desire to share such sensitive information, and had made time for them to discuss difficult issues. Such sharing might bring greater closeness between the carer and the young person, enable confidences to be shared and help the young person to integrate past painful events.

Responding to the child's emotional age

One particular aspect of sensitive responding that, in itself, was related to the success of adolescent foster placements was the carer's ability to respond to the child's emotional age. Many adolescents in foster care show evidence of behaviour more suited to younger children, while others appear to be functioning at a more mature level (Farmer and Pollock, 1998; Farmer et al., 2004; Lipscombe, 2006). This may of course also be a problem for younger children, but the discrepancy between chronological age and emotional age is likely to be more apparent and more extreme for older children. There were fewer disruptions when foster carers had been able to respond to the child's emotional age as well as their chronological age. For example, one 15 year old whose mother had died when he was 9 desperately missed physical attention. Although the carer said she felt uncomfortable with it, she allowed him to have a cuddle and suck his thumb for a while, as a younger child would, before encouraging him to act in a more age-appropriate manner. Such responsiveness indicates sensitivity to the need of many of these young people to rework some of their earlier missed developmental experiences, for example for children's play activities and nurture, and a willingness to supply some of these in the placement. It implies tolerance and understanding that looked after adolescents who may appear superficially street-wise and 'mature' may need a regular opportunity to regress in their behaviour, alongside the more general routine of age-appropriate activities and relationships. This has implications for the training needed by carers and suggests the need for a greater focus on child development and an increase in awareness of the potential disparity between a child's chronological age and their emotional or developmental age.

Facilitation of education

As with many children within the care system (Jackson, 1994; Borland et al., 1998; Harker et al., 2003; Social Exclusion Unit, 2003; Taylor, 2006), the majority of the young people in this study had experienced high levels of educational disruption and had low levels of educational attainment. A lack of educational skills makes care-leavers particularly vulnerable to unemployment and is associated with involvement in offending behaviour and social exclusion (Farrington, 1996; Taylor, 2006). Section 52 of the Children Act 2004 places a statutory duty on local authorities to promote the educational attainment of looked after children, and the Green Paper (Department for Education and Skills, 2006) placed education at its centre. Both of these were written after this research was concluded. However, it appears that the implementation of both Section 52 and the proposals within the Green Paper may be difficult to achieve. For example, although the majority of the foster carers in the study were highly or fairly involved in facilitating the young person's education, encouraging the young person to attend school and showing interest in their achievements, 14% were not. We found that single carers were less involved than others in young people's education, probably because of time pressures associated with their higher levels of workforce participation, combined with lower levels of training and support. In addition, Jackson (2007) suggests that carers who are not involved in young people's schooling might not accept the promotion of education as being part of their role and, furthermore, that social workers might be reluctant to place pressure on the carers to support the child's education for fear of losing the placements. For this reason, the plans in the White Paper to emphasize educational support in training for foster carers and in the National Minimum Standards for fostering services are very welcome.

Placements in our study were more likely to break down if the young person had low confidence in their school work. As Taylor (2006) argues, looked after children too frequently have to move schools when they move placements (see also Sinclair, 2005); these children may find that their coursework is disrupted (which is particularly problematic for those studying for GCSEs) – an issue which has been taken up in the White Paper - and they may lose confidence in their achievements. It is likely that providing additional support, encouragement and assistance to these teenagers could increase their confidence levels and enhance placement stability as well as helping to maximise their educational progress and employment opportunities (see also Jackson and Ajayi, 2007). Taylor (2006) also found that developing new skills, making new friendships and joining new groups at school could help prevent young people from truanting, social exclusion and involvement in offending behaviour. The range of proposals in the White Paper to support the education of looked after children, including a much greater emphasis in social work training on the importance of education and social relationships, is therefore very welcome. Social workers need to be actively involved in organising educational support for young people and ensuring that foster carers are also highly involved, and that their mutual roles are clear. Both also require education departments to provide suitable school placements and referrals for more specialist help in a much more timely way than has been the case in the past. It will be interesting to see how far new joint structures for children's services and education facilitate this.

Facilitation of friendships and activities

Establishing and maintaining good peer relationships is an important aspect of adolescent emotional and behavioural development, yet many young people in care have problematic peer relationships (Hodges and Tizard, 1989; Quinton et al., 1998). The development of positive relationships and activities is important for the promotion of self-esteem and confidence, can help to expand the opportunities available to young people and promote resilience (eg Gilligan, 2000, 2001). Furthermore participating in hobbies and activities can contribute to educational progress for children in care, by encouraging engagement with prosocial adults and by the implicit learning opportunities (Gilligan, 2007).

Interestingly, young people who, at the outset of the placement, had difficulties in making and maintaining adequate peer relationships had significantly fewer disruptions and more successful placements than those who had positive peer relationships. These teenagers had either no friends or, whilst good at making initial contact with other children, could not sustain the relationship. Some sought the company of younger or much older children, or established exclusive relationships with the opposite sex, which excluded them from 'normal' peer relationships. The foster carers needed to provide these young people with one to one nurturing to help them overcome their previous dysfunctional relationships and to develop a positive relationship with caring adults, before assisting them to develop their peer relationships.

The research findings further showed that young people who had some special skills or interests of their own were significantly more likely to have good quality placements than those who did not. Young people who spend their time in positive activities also have less time to become involved in anti-social behaviour. In addition, carers who are involved and interested in young people's free time are likely to have more awareness of their activities outside the home and thus have more ability to supervise them outside the placement. Many of the young people did not see themselves as requiring assistance with activities which may have deterred the carers from helping. However, over half of the carers were involved in arranging or suggesting activities for the young people. Carers need to be encouraged and supported to view the fostering task holistically and to consider the management of the young people's friendships and activities outside the placement as an integral element of their role.

Promoting sexual health and relationships

As adolescence is typically a time of increasing sexual awareness and sexual activity, carers have an important part to play in promoting fostered adolescents' sexual health and relationships (Knight et al., 2006). However, this proved to be a more problematic area of parenting and a significant proportion (20%) of the carers had little or no knowledge of the young person's relationships. Over half of the foster carers were concerned about the young people's sexual relationships, but few actually talked to them about their concerns. Two fifths of the carers did not discuss sexual health and sexuality with the young person, and they were less at ease discussing sexual matters with boys than girls. Many looked after young people are poorly informed about normal sexual development, sexual health or contraception (see, for example, Farmer and Pollock, 1998) and need the opportunity to talk about these issues and their relationships. There was considerable confusion over whose responsibility it was to talk to the young people about sex and sexual health. Some carers believed (or had been told) that the social worker would assume this responsibility, yet this was not happening. The high levels of young people leaving care who are either pregnant or who already have children (Corylon and McGuire, 1997; Haydon,, 2003) is testament to the fact that these young people may need greater advice or support in managing their sexual relationships. The need for sexual health and relationship advice to be included in residential and foster carer training is recognised in the White Paper. However, it is equally important that foster carers (or others nominated to help) feel empowered and supported to take on this responsibility. In addition, young people with backgrounds of sexual abuse may need more specialist help to address these issues (Farmer and Pollock, 1998).

Developing independence

Parents and carers of adolescents have to maintain a balance between ensuring young people's personal safety and enhancing the development of their autonomy, particularly as they start to prepare for independent living (Walker et al., 2002). Suitable boundaries for the young people need to be established so that their behaviour can be contained, without being too restrictive or permissive, taking into account their developmental and emotional age. Judging where to set the boundaries for looked after adolescents is sometimes very difficult. The study suggests that in some ways it is the reverse of normal child development where boundaries are established early and gradually relaxed as the child grows. Many of these teenagers had not had consistent boundaries set before and some were unaccustomed to any restrictions on their behaviour. We found that in the latter situations foster carers made most progress if they set a few loose boundaries to begin with and then gradually established more boundaries to bring the young person into a more normative range – at the same time as encouraging the young person to become independent.

Integral to establishing appropriate boundaries is the supervision of the young person, the awareness of where the adolescent is, who they are with and what they are doing. Adolescents, partly as a result of their stage of development, may be more likely than younger children, to succumb to environmental pressures to engage in activities of which adults disapprove. Good supervision outside the home was linked to improved placement outcomes and is important in keeping young people safe in terms of involvement in offending, prostitution, drug and alcohol misuse, and sexually high risk behaviour. Carers were more likely to increase their supervision within the home if they were concerned about the young person's use of drugs or alcohol, but not outside the home. This suggests that the carers' increased concern may be related to the protection of their own children or other fostered children, or it may be that the carers do not see their role as extending to supervision outside the placement. Carers can more easily have an influence within the home and the young people are likely to be more amenable to control within this placement setting than outside it. However, these young people are often at risk outside and it may be that there are opportunities for carers to extend their monitoring role, for example by offering lifts, talking to the young people about their friends and intervening if children make contact with high risk individuals (see also Farmer and Pollock, 1998; Stace and Lowe, 2007; Lowe et al, 2007).

All young people need to develop self-care and life skills to enable a successful transition to independent living. However, for many looked after adolescents, a return home will not be envisaged and they may have to become self-sufficient and independent at an earlier age than other teenagers

(Walker et al., 2002; Sinclair et al., 2004b; Sinclair, 2005). Despite the plans in the White Paper that children will be entitled to remain in care until they are 21, some may decide to live on their own before then (Taylor, 2006) and need to be supported to do so. Young people who have not been looked after have the option of returning home should independent living become problematic; this not always possible for looked after children. Carers need to find a balance between encouraging the development of life skills and self-efficacy whilst enabling the young person to feel settled and secure in the foster family. In our study, carers who involved the young people in an average level of preparation for leaving care were significantly more likely to provide good quality placements for the young person overall compared with those who involved the young people in either little or high levels of preparation. Not helping the young person develop life skills would put them at a disadvantage when they left care but perhaps too much of an emphasis on independence meant that the young person did not settle as well within the placement or that the placements was never seen as more than a short-term bridge to independence.

Supporting adolescent foster placements

Social workers and others supporting adolescent foster placements need to be aware that the quality of parenting provided by the carers can be adversely affected in certain circumstances. For example, foster carers' ability to parent the fostered young people decreased when the carers were experiencing significant stress or when the fostered adolescents had a negative impact on other children within the household (Lipscombe et al., 2003, 2004). Social workers need not only to be aware of the stresses and strains carers often experience when caring for teenagers, but also to provide effective and timely support, including arranging the provision of appropriate therapeutic help for young people when it is needed. Furthermore, planning and preparation for the placements is critical for both the foster carers and the young people to ensure that the placement begins in a positive manner, that a package of support is in place and, in addition, partnership working is needed with the foster carers to pro-actively manage the young people's contact with birth family members.

Preparation for placement

The practice and research literature lays considerable emphasis on the importance of preparation of children for placement and of giving adequate information to carers (Farmer and Pollock, 1998; Quinton et al., 1998; Triseliotis et al., 2000; Sinclair, 2005). Our research suggests that adequate preparation can make a real difference to outcomes for adolescents: placements in which the young person felt that they had been given adequate information about the carers and their family before the move were more likely to be rated as successful and were less likely to break down. However, a third of the young people said that they had not been consulted about the move, and a third had not had an opportunity to meet their carers before moving to the placement. Furthermore, two-fifths of the carers said that there was information about the young person that they had needed and did not have and almost a quarter had been given information that was neither accurate nor up to date. There was a tendency for social workers to give less information about the children with the more disturbed behaviour, yet there were significantly fewer disruptions when the young people had been no more difficult to manage than the carers had expected. This suggests that, within certain parameters, foster carers may be able to manage difficult adolescents as long as they take them with full knowledge of their difficulties. It is clearly also critical to provide full information to the carers to prevent high risk adolescents from being placed in situations where they pose risks to other children in the family, for example as a result of sexually abusing or aggressive and violent behaviour.

Foster carer strain

Where foster carers had experienced a high number of stressful events (such as bereavements, relationship difficulties, illness or financial worries) prior to the placement there was an increased risk of disruption (Farmer et al., 2005). Strain was also particularly evident during the placements when the carers had only accepted the placed young person with reluctance, or under some pressure, or if the adolescent had considerable behaviour problems, including conduct disorder and hyperactivity. The link between an accumulation of stress and higher levels of placement breakdown may in part relate to the lower levels of positive parenting shown by these carers and their reduced capacity to ensure that the young people's needs were met (for example for appropriate education or counselling). Carers under strain responded less sensitively to the young people, were less able to respond to their emotional age, and gave little attention to preparing them for independence. Strained carers also felt less supported than others; these carers significantly more often than others found the children's social workers difficult to contact and more often felt that their views were not taken seriously by the professionals involved with the young person. Family placement workers must therefore assess the level of strain carers are under before a placement is even made, and also be alert for signs that carers are under strain during the placement so that they can intervene before the capacity to care for the young person deteriorates.

Contact with birth family members

The ability to parent the fostered young person could also be undermined by the influence of the birth family. Whilst contact for all looked after children is a complex phenomenon (see, for example, Sinclair et al., 2004a; Moyers et al., 2006), there is a widespread idea that, because of their age, adolescents can manage the practicalities of contact for themselves and that foster carers and social workers need to be less involved in arrangements (Sinclair, 2005).

In this research, however, contact for the majority of adolescents was often very problematic and was one of a number of factors that led to placement breakdown. At the start of the placement a third of the foster carers felt that the contact arrangements were not in the best interests of the young people, and almost half considered that the young person placed with them had difficulties in their contact with family members (Moyers et al., 2006). Typical difficulties were continued rejection, unreliability, neglect and abuse by parents during contact. Furthermore, birth family contact could undermine the influence of the foster carers, particularly if family members encouraged anti-social or risk-taking behaviour. At the one year follow-up, almost two thirds of the young people had contact with someone who was rated by the researchers as detrimental to them, and a third had no beneficial contact with anyone.

Legal arrangements did not always protect young people who were determined to keep in contact with family member. Even if it was prohibited or if the foster carer or social worker thought it was not in the child's best interests, some of the children themselves chose to maintain contact. For example, one 15 year old boy made many visits to his mother at her home, even though his violent step-father was there and subjected him to numerous physical assaults. These adolescents may need additional work to help them understand their family relationships, to negotiate appropriate contact, and to keep themselves safe if they are determined to keep in touch.

The difficulties encountered by young people whose contact was not supervised were not always apparent to their social workers. Many of the foster carers were in a good position to observe the effects of contact on the young people they looked after, and regular discussion between the social worker and foster carers would assist in keeping matters under review. In those cases where social workers took action, changes usually resulted in definite improvements for the young people and their placements. The changes were often quite small adjustments to the frequency and duration of meetings, or the involvement of other more positive relatives (see also Marsh and Peel, 1999). While there may be limits on how far long-standing relationship patterns between children and their birth parents can be changed, the negotiation of meaningful contact is an important task and more work with young people is needed to assist them to understand and manage their relationships with family members more effectively. When negative relationship patterns persist, young people need help in integrating the reality of their parents' actions and in dealing with their own experiences of rejection and loss in ways that allow them to move on, build up a sense of self-worth in spite of these experiences and make use of other more sustaining relationships. Their ability to form and maintain healthy adult relationships is likely to be seriously jeopardised if they are not given assistance in dealing with these issues.

Placement support and services

It was clear that, for the foster carers, appropriate help for the young people was a crucial strand in their overall support systems. Over a third of the young people were seeing a specialist for counselling and carers tended to feel better supported when this was the case. Conversely, when foster carers considered that a young person needed specialist help and it was not provided, this did much to make them feel unsupported. Over and above this, there were fewer disruptions when appropriate therapeutic help was provided for young people (or was not needed) and more successful placements when young people reported that they were receiving such assistance. There were more disruptions when carers had felt the need to seek mental health help for the young person but had been unable to locate such assistance.

Foster carers who were looking after teenagers with either conduct problems or hyperactivity had great difficulty in coping with these young people on their own without support services (see also Quinton et al., 1998). A significant proportion of these carers had asked for help, primarily for the young people but also for themselves, but most had received either no assistance at all or a service that was inadequate or insufficiently tailored to the needs of the young people and their carers. Clearly, young people who have severe behaviour problems or are hyperactive require intensive packages of support if their placements are to survive.

Carers who had a lot of support from their own children (including adult children) had fewer placement disruptions, as did those who received substantial support from other family members (principally their parents and/or partners). In addition, there were significantly more successful placements when the carers were supported by their social networks and local professionals, such as doctors and teachers. Placements were more often successful when the social workers had arranged some services for the young people, and importantly support from the young people's social workers themselves was significantly related to the success of the placement. The intention in the White Paper to use weekly foster carer meetings and the Parent Reports on young people's behaviour (from the MTFC) in order to identify and focus services on the placements most vulnerable to disruption could prove useful, particularly as we found that foster carers under the most strain received the fewest social work visits.

Implications for policy and practice

The placement outcomes in this study show that adolescents with considerable emotional and behavioural difficulties can be successfully placed in mainstream and specialist foster care placements and not all will need the high levels of support provided in MTFC placements. Indeed, it is of note that the behavioural, emotional and educational difficulties experienced by these young people reflect those experienced by the young people placed in MTFC (Roberts, 2006), and the overall success rate of these placements is not dissimilar. A third (31%) of the children placed in MTFC were classified as 'early leavers', with their placements having disrupted, compared with 40% of those in our study.

Foster carers within mainstream and specialist schemes can provide high levels of positive parenting for adolescents if sufficient training and support is provided, and if the parameters of the foster carer's role are clearly and unambiguously delineated. In particular, placement outcomes for adolescents are likely to be improved if foster carers are trained to: respond to the young people's emotional and developmental age; talk to young people about the past and about difficulties in their relationships with their families; monitor adolescents' activities outside the home (see also Stace and Lowe, 2007); and assist young people to develop independence and autonomy whilst also providing them with a secure base. Furthermore, foster carers need to be encouraged to view their role as extending beyond the boundaries of the home to facilitate the young people's education, activities and peer relationships.

Whilst Jackson (2007) argues that some foster carers do not see their role as encompassing the facilitation of education, the consultation responses to the Green Paper suggest that more responsibility for promoting children's education could be invested in the carers themselves. However, to enable carers to take on this role they will need further training to help them to understand the educational system and in supporting learning at home (including through leisure activities and hobbies), as recommended in the White Paper. In addition, an examination of any specific barriers to single carers being fully involved in education would be useful. Regular contact between the school and the carer is critical and schools need to reciprocate the carer's commitment to young people. Social workers and foster carers need to be clear about their respective responsibilities with regard to schooling, for example who should arrange meetings with the school or attend parents' evenings (Sinclair, 2005). It is also important that education departments become much more active in providing suitable educational placements for children who are looked after and in sustaining the education of children at risk of school exclusion. For placements where there is no educational provision at all, an education worker could be assigned to help the carer access education on the behalf of the young person (see also Walker et al., 2002), a model that is routine and works well in some independent fostering agencies. The range of policy changes in the White Paper which address education could make a real difference to the capacity of placements to contain young people as well as to their educational experiences while in care.

Clarity is needed as to who has responsibility for some areas of parenting that have particular relevance to adolescents, for example whether foster carers or social workers have responsibility to promote the young person's sexual health and safe and positive sexual relationships. Whilst the White Paper addresses the training needs of foster carers in this area and some professionals suggest that the young person should be able to talk to the person with whom they feel most comfortable (Knight et al., 2006), we would argue that there needs to be a nominated person (arguably foster carers since the young person will have most contact with them) who ensures that the young person has had the opportunity to discuss sexual health, contraception and relationships, even if they choose to discuss these issues with someone else.

Social workers and foster carers also need to work together to help the young person negotiate and manage appropriate birth family contact. Adolescents are more able to take the initiative in arranging contact with their birth family than are younger children, yet this can expose them to unsatisfactory and sometimes harmful contact. Social workers in Cleaver's study (2000) had limited time for work relating to contact, and this is an area where foster carers could take on more responsibility, particularly as we found that they were often more aware of ongoing contact issues than the social worker. Cleaver (2000) found that carers who had formal training on contact were more likely to have established positive relationships with parents and to be involved in contact arrangements.

In the study, high quality support from social workers and other professionals was related to less strain for foster carers and to better parenting skills and so to better placement outcomes. Good social work support for placements is arguably one of the major contributions of independent fostering agencies (Farmer et al., 2007). For this to occur in local authorities as well, children's social workers in particular need the kinds of caseloads and team structures that would allow them to give due time to looked after young people and their carers. In addition, therapeutic help is important for some young people and helps to support their placements. Thus, improved support and services for foster carers and young people are crucial elements in improved services.

Whilst the White Paper has included policy changes in many of the areas mentioned, the details of many are awaited. It is not always clear how proposals will be resourced or how real leverage can be brought to bear in some key areas, for example, in providing better access to counselling and mental health services for looked after young people, or in improving the support and services available to foster carers. Nonetheless, it is to be hoped that local authorities will seize the initiative provided by the White Paper. Addressing the specific needs of fostered adolescents and their carers will help to sustain the placements of the majority of young people in care who will not have access to highly specialised treatment foster care.

References

Aldgate, J., Maluccio, A., and Reeves, C. (1989) Adolescents in foster families: An overview. in J. Aldgate, A. Maluccio, and C. Reeves (Eds.) *Adolescents in Foster Families*. London: Batsford

A National Voice (2005) *No Place Like Home*. Manchester: A National Voice

Barnardos (2006) *Failed by the System*. Ilford: Barnardos

Berridge, D. (1997) *Foster Care: A research review*. London: TSO

Borland, M., Pearson, C., Hill, M., Tisdall, K., and Bloomfield, I. (1998) *Education and Care away from Home*. Edinburgh: Scottish Council for Research in Education

Cleaver, H. (2000) *Fostering Family Contact: A study of children, parents and foster carers*. London: The Stationery Office

Corylon, J. and McGuire, C. (1997). *Young Parents in Public Care: Pregnancy and parenthood among young people looked after by local authorities*. London: National Children's Bureau

Department for Education and Skills (2006) *Care Matters: Transforming the lives of children and young people in care*. Green Paper Cm. 6932. London: TSO

Department for Education and Skills (2007) *Care Matters: Time for change*. Cm. 7137. London: TSO

Downes, C. (1992) *Separation Revisited: Adolescents in foster family care*. Aldershot: Ashgate

Farmer, E. and Moyers, S. (forthcoming). *Kinship Care: Fostering effective family and friends placements*. London, Jessica Kingsley

Farmer, E. and Pollock, S. (1998) *Sexually Abused and Sexually Abusing Children in Substitute Care.* Chichester: John Wiley

Farmer, E., Moyers, S., and Lipscombe, J. (2004) *Fostering Adolescents.* London: Jessica Kingsley

Farmer E., Lipscombe J., and Moyers S. (2005) Foster carer strain and its impact on parenting and placement outcomes for adolescents. *British Journal of Social Work,* 35, 237-253

Farmer E., Selwyn J., Quinton D., Saunders H., Staines J., Turner W., and Meakings S. (2007) *Children Placed with FCA: Experiences and progress 12 months on.* Final Report to FCA, Hadley Centre for Adoption and Foster Care Studies. Bristol: University of Bristol, School for Policy Studies

Farrington, D. (1996) *Understanding and Preventing Youth Crime.* York: Joseph Rowntree Foundation

Gilligan, R. (2000) Adversity, resilience and young people: The protective value of positive school and spare time experiences. *Children and Society,* 14, 1, 37-47

Gilligan, R. (2001) *Promoting Resilience: A resource guild on working with children in the care system.* London, BAAF

Gilligan, R. (2007) Spare time activities for young people in care: what can they contribute to educational progress?, *Adoption and Fostering,* 31, 1 92-99

Harker, M., Dobel-Ober, D., Lawrence, J., Berridge, D., and Sinclair, R. (2003) Who takes care of education? Looked after children's perceptions of support for educational progress. *Child & Family Social Work,* 8, 2, 89-100

Haydon, D. (2003). *Teenage Pregnancy and Looked After Children / Care Leavers.* Resource for Teenage Pregnancy Co-ordinators. Ilford: Barnardos

Hodges, J. and Tizard, B. (1989) Social and family relationships of ex-institutional adolescents. *Journal of Child Psychology and Psychiatry,* 30, 77-97

Jackson, S. (1994) Educating children in residential and foster care, *Oxford Review of Education,* 20, 3, 267-279

Jackson, S (2001) *Nobody Ever Told us School Mattered: Raising the educational attainments of children in care.* London: BAAF

Jackson, S. (2007) Progress at last? Guest Editorial to special issue, Education. *Adoption and Fostering,* 31, 1,3-5

Jackson S. and Ajayi S. (2007) Foster care and higher education. *Adoption and Fostering,* 31, 1, 62-72

Jones, G. and Wallace, C. (1992) *Youth, Family and Citizenship.* Buckingham: Open University Press

Knight, A., Chase, E., and Aggleton, P. (2006) Teenage pregnancy among young people in and leaving care: Messages and implications for foster care, *Adoption and Fostering Journal,* 30, 1, 58-69

Lipscombe, J. (2006) *Care or Control? Foster care for young people on remand.* London: British Association for Adoption and Fostering

Lipscombe, J., Farmer, E., and Moyers, S. (2003) Parenting fostered adolescents: skills and strategies. *Child and Family Social Work,* 8, 4, 243-255

Lipscombe, J., Moyers, S., and Farmer, E. (2004) What changes in parenting' approaches occur over the course of adolescent foster care placements? *Child and Family Social Work*, 9, 347-357

Lowe, K., Hellett, L.J., and Stace, S. (2007) *Teenagers in Foster Care: promoting positive relationships. A training course.* Brighton: Trust for the Study of Adolescence

Marsh P. and Peel M. (1999) *Leaving Care in Partnership: Family involvement with care leavers..* London: TSO

Moyers, S., Farmer, E., and Lipscombe, J. (2006) Contact with family members and its impact on adolescents and their foster placements,. *British Journal of Social Work*, 36, 541-559

Packman, J. and Hall, C. (1998) *From Care to Accommodation. Support, protection and control in child care services.* London: SO

Quinton D., Rushton A., Dance C.,, and Mayes D. (1998) *Joining New Families: A study of adoption and fostering in middle childhood.* Chichester: John Wiley

Roberts, R. (2006) *Multidimensional Treatment Foster Care In England.* Second Annual Report.London: Department for Education and Skills

Social Exclusion Unit (2003), *A Better Education for Children in Care.* London: Social Exclusion Unit / Office of the Deputy Prime Minister

Sinclair, I. (2005) *Fostering Now: Messages from research.* London: Jessica Kingsley

Sinclair, R., Garnett, L., and Berridge, D. (1995) *Social Work and Assessment with Adolescents.*London: National Children's Bureau

Sinclair, I., Gibbs, I., and Wilson K. (2004a) *Foster Placements: Why they succeed and why they fail.* London: Jessica Kingsley Publishers

Sinclair, I., Baker, C., Wilson, K., and Gibbs, I. (2004b) *Foster Children: Where they go and how they get on.* London: Jessica Kingsley

Stace, S. and Lowe, K. (2007) *Reducing Risks for Young People in Foster Care: A UK study.* Brighton: Trust for the Study of Adolescence

Taylor, C. (2006) *Young People in Care and Criminal Behaviour.* London: Jessica Kingsley

Thoburn, J., Norford, L., and Parvez Rashid, S. (2000) *Permanent Family Placement for Children of Minority Ethnic Origin.* London: Jessica Kingsley Publishers

Triseliotis, J., Borland, M., Hill, M., and Lambert, L.(1995) *Teenagers and the Social Work Services.* London: HMSO

Walker, M., Hill, M., and Triseliotis, J. (2002) *Testing the Limits of Foster Care: Fostering as an alternative to secure accommodation.* London: British Association for Adoption and Fostering

Ward, H. (Ed.) (1995) *Looking After Children: Research into practice.* The Second Report to the Department of Health on Assessing Outcomes in Child Care. London: HMSO

10
Obstacles to participation in education, employment and training for young people leaving care

Jo Dixon

Introduction

Research over the past three decades has consistently shown that many care leavers face difficulties and disadvantage as they embark upon participation in education, employment and training (EET) (Stein and Carey, 1986; Biehal et al., 1995; Broad, 1998; Dixon and Stein, 2005). Most encounter obstacles to finding and sustaining career options in the early years after care and for some this can persist into adulthood, leading to an increased risk of long-term unemployment and social exclusion (Cheung and Heath, 1994).

In response, we have seen an increased legislative and policy focus. Maximising opportunities for care-experienced young people over the age of sixteen years is a key part of the current leaving care agenda. It is reflected in the Children Leaving Care Act 2000 (CLCA), performance assessment framework (PAF) targets and both the Green Paper, Care Matters (DfES, 2006d) and the White Paper, Care Matters: Time for Change (DfES, 2007) which draw particular attention to the disparity between care-experienced youth and their non-care peers in, amongst other things, schooling and post-16 participation. These developments include increased provision for career support as part of pathway planning through the CLCA and the introduction of targets for local authorities to maximise the numbers of looked after children achieving educational success and the number of care leavers participating in employment, education and training (EET). Additionally, we have seen the development of mainstream initiatives to tackle youth unemployment and non-participation such as The New Deal for young people, Education Maintenance Allowance (EMA) and increased training and education options.

Against this background, this chapter draws on research findings (Dixon et al., 2006) to explore the extent to which young people continue to experience obstacles as they leave care and begin the journey into education, employment and training. It will show that, for the research sample at least, progress towards reducing the disparity between care leavers and their non-care peers in term of participation and removing the obstacles to sustaining participation has been slow. The chapter considers the nature of these obstacles, locating them within young people's past and current experiences, the leaving care context and within normative youth transitions and labour market frameworks.

Drawing upon the experiences of the study sample, the chapter also explores the factors that facilitate successful career outcomes after leaving care and those which impede positive progress. It also highlights current strategies for supporting care leavers to maximise their potential and opportunities and for reducing the *'significant and widening gap'* (DfES, 2006d, p.5.) between outcomes for care-experienced young people and their non-care peers.

The study and research sample

The study, which was commissioned by the DfES, took place across seven English local authorities during 2001-2003. The participating authorities represented a broad geographical spread and included London boroughs, shire counties, metropolitan councils and a unitary authority. The key focus of the research was to explore the costs and outcomes associated with leaving care under the CLCA. In doing so, it looked at young people's experiences of the transition from care to independent adult living, and identified aspects of their in-care and post-care experiences that offered protective factors or posed risks for successful outcomes. It also looked at the ways that support from professionals, family and friends helped young people to achieve more positive outcomes.

Baseline interviews were conducted with 106 young people approximately two months after leaving care. Follow-up interviews were conducted ten to twelve months later to find out how they were progressing. Parallel information was collected from each young person's personal adviser (PA) and policy interviews were carried out with senior managers. Data included a range of quantitative measures as well as more open ended, qualitative material. Questionnaires and interview schedules facilitated the collection of information on young people's care careers, transitional support arrangements and initial post-care outcomes and progress in key life areas (e.g. housing, education, career, mental and physical health and well-being); the support available from family, friends and carers; and the use made of professional support services.

Outcome information related to the first 12–15 months after care. In this sense the study provided a sharp focus on the early stages of the transition from care. The findings, therefore, represent intermediate outcomes, which are indicative of the initial progress being made by young people on their journey to adulthood. A range of statistical tests was used to analyse outcomes. Some results have been reported in this paper[1].

The sample was broadly representative of the general care leaver population. A similar proportion of young men (47%) and women (53%) took part in the study and one quarter was from minority ethnic backgrounds (25%). Just under half of the sample (44%) was considered by practitioners to have mental health, emotional or behavioural difficulties and 17% were considered to have a sensory, physical or learning impairment. Although the majority of young people (69%) had last entered care as teenagers; more than two-fifths (43%) had been looked after for five or more years. Over half (59%) had left care from a foster placement and 41% had left from residential or other placements, however, most had experienced a range of care placements throughout their care career. All, but one of the young people in the sample, were aged 16-18 at recruitment to the study. This age-range represents an important stage with respect to career paths, where decisions and trajectories embarked upon often lay the foundations for future choices and destinations (Banks et al., 1992).

While drawing upon the wider findings of the study, this paper will focus primarily on young people's experiences of post-16 participation in EET, in the year or so after leaving care.

Participation in EET

The transition to adulthood is a time of opportunities, challenges and choices. Some young people make a successful transition from care, settling into stable post-care living and succeeding in their chosen career options whilst others make steady progress with help from support networks and professionals. However, a significant number of those more vulnerable young people face an enduring struggle. Past research has highlighted post-16 participation as a particular area of disadvantage and difficulty for many care leavers, with unemployment and over representation in low paid, unskilled occupations featuring prominently in the leaving care literature (Biehal et al., 1995; Broad, 1998; Stein, 2004).

Despite an increasing policy focus on the problem, it remains that many young people continue to experience difficulties in finding a foothold on the career ladder in the early years after care. The national picture currently shows that, when considered alongside wider patterns of youth participation, care leavers are far less likely to be engaged in education, employment and training. This was clearly evident within our study where participation rates were low and despite around half having entered education, employment or training at some point over the follow-up, most young people struggled to sustain participation and many drifted in and out of periods of inactivity. Before considering the reasons for low participation it is worth considering more closely, the extent to which it affects care leavers by looking at the different participation rates and outcomes.

Participation rates for the study sample as a whole are shown in table 1. Further analysis of individual experiences showed that there was evidence of career instability over the follow-up with 43% moving between the different career status groups.

Education

In terms of education participation, there was some indication of an increase in the number of care leavers engaging in post-compulsory education. Around one third (35%) of the sample was undertaking some form of education. This represents an increase on figures reported in past research and reflects the findings of a contemporary survey of care leavers that noted a general increase in education participation from 19% in 1994 to 31% in 2003 (Broad, 2003).

This rise in education participation may be driven by a combination of wider factors including general trends in mainstream youth career options, which have seen an increase in further education opportunities. It also reflects stronger links between leaving care services and agencies such as Connexions as well as the impact of increased financial support through specific funding under the CLCA for education assistance and discretionary incentives based on attendance and progress, as well as mainstream support through the EMA. It is also likely that the need to meet government targets for maximising participation is providing a sharper focus for professionals working with care-experienced and unemployed youth.

Whilst increased education participation is to be welcomed, and our findings certainly give cause for optimism, there was equally cause for caution. First, it was apparent from our research that sustaining participation was a challenge and required careful management and support in the months after care. Only half of those in education at baseline were still in education a year on from care and overall, the number of young people in education had fallen from 35% to 23% at follow-up.

Table 1

Young people's career status and progress

Career status group	Baseline (%) (n=106)	Follow-up (%) (n=101)
Unemployed	43	44
Full-time education	27	21
Part-time education	8	2
Training	8	6
Caring for child	7	8
Full-time employment	4	10
Part-time employment	2	3
Custody	1	1
Lost to follow-up	0	5

Career outcome - progress overtime	(%)
Improved	15
Remained good	31
Deteriorated	20
Remained poor	34

Whilst some had completed their studies there was strong anecdotal evidence of early dropout due to personal circumstance and difficulties. Reports from young people and their PAs highlighted problems around debt, ability and emotional issues. There was also evidence that some young people had been encouraged to participate in unsuitable courses, which did not meet their needs, abilities or interests.

Second, despite the increase in the number of care leavers in post-compulsory education, there remained a significant disparity when compared to participation rates for school leavers in general. Government figures (DfES, 2005) report 72% of 16 year olds, 60% of 17 year olds and 39% of 18 year olds are in full-time education; far higher than the 35% of 16–18 year olds in the current study who were in full or part-time education. Additionally, significantly fewer care leavers attend University (1% compared to 38% of the wider population (Jackson et al., 2003). This was mirrored in the current study where only one young person was attending University.

Training

A similar picture emerged for participation in training. Less than one in ten young people in the study had undertaken a training course in the initial period after care. Again, whilst some had completed their training course during the follow-up timescale there was evidence of attrition due to early dropout. Moreover, training did not appear to increase the chances of employment, in the short-term at least, with almost two-thirds (63%) of those involved in training being unemployed a year on from care. Training rates were also comparatively low in relation to national figures, which indicate that 75% of 16–18 year olds were engaged in training or education (DfES, 2005). The equivalent combined figure for the study group was 29%.

Employment

Employment rates for care leavers were also low with only 10% of the sample in full-time work a year on from care. This corresponds to findings from recent studies of care leavers in Northern Ireland (Pinkerton and McCrea, 1999), Scotland (Dixon and Stein, 2005) and England (Broad, 2003). Furthermore, where young people were employed, there was evidence of marginal, insecure employment, either on a temporary, casual or 'cash in hand' basis.

This may well reflect wider youth labour market patterns, which show a general decline in the tendency to move straight from school to work as wider transitional opportunities become available and which have resulted in lower numbers in employment within the 16-18 age-group generally. Nevertheless, care experienced young people appear less likely than their non-care peers to be in employment. Recent national participation rates for 18 year olds in England and Wales show that almost a third (31%) had a full-time or part-time job (DfES, 2006c), indicating that those with experience of care face greater challenges.

Unemployment and non-participation

Unsurprisingly, given the relatively low participation rates, unemployment featured prominently for care leavers in our study. More than two-fifths were unemployed at baseline and a year after leaving care. When full-time parents were taken into account, the number not in education, employment or training (NEET) rose to 56% at follow-up.

Of course, levels of non-participation amongst care leavers cannot be disconnected from wider social and economic trends affecting young people in general, which have seen the youth labour market becoming increasingly competitive with the rise in demand for an educated and specialised workforce. However, alongside this have arisen a number of developments to address youth participation rates such as the introduction of Connexions; the promotion of a more co-ordinated approach to post-16 education and training through the Learning and Skills Councils; and the growth of schemes such as Modern Apprenticeships and the New Deal. Also, the increased commitment to financial support for young people through the

EMA and for care leavers in education, training or employment through the CLCA should establish participation in EET as a more accessible and viable option. However, as findings from this and other sources show, progress to date, has been slow. For example, the most recent national statistics suggest a steady increase in overall participation amongst the care leaver group to 63% of those still in touch with the local authority at the age of nineteen years (DfES, 2006a). Despite this, they remain considerably disadvantaged in terms of post-16 participation when compared to their non-care peers. Although statistics vary, care leavers are between three and five times more likely than their non-care peers to be NEET (DfES, 2003) with around 47% of care leavers nationally classed as NEET compared to around 10% of all young people in the 16-18 age- group.

To understand why care leavers experience difficulties and disparity in post-16 participation we need to consider the nature of the obstacles that impede their progress and obscure the opportunities available to them. A key focus of our own research involved looking at young people who were doing well and those who were doing less well to identify which factors assisted participation and positive outcomes and those that hindered success.[2]

Obstacles to participation

Understanding and locating the factors associated with non-participation can inform the development of support to help young people maximise their potential, overcome obstacles and achieve economic and overall well-being.

The causes of non-participation arise from multiple difficulties and disadvantage affecting the lives of those more vulnerable groups within society. For care leavers, many will encounter challenges to participation as a consequence of their pre-care, in-care and post-care experiences.

Pre-care

Although the remit of the study prevented a focus on the pre-care experience of the sample, we know from exiting research that many children entering care do so with a legacy of disadvantage that can predispose them to poor career outcomes (Stein, 2004). The difficulties and experiences that brought them into care; early loss or trauma, poor parenting, family problems and disadvantage can have a lasting impact, particularly where needs are not subsequently addressed.

Studies of unemployment within the wider population meanwhile, show that socio-economic disadvantage can shape future life chances. Parental background has been identified as a factor in economic activity and living in council rented accommodation, having neither parent in full-time work or parents in manual occupations increases the likelihood of non-participation (DfES, 2000). Similarly, Bynner and Parson's (2002) identified parental income as the greatest predictor of education outcomes and thereby subsequent success in the labour market.

These factors are particularly relevant to care leavers, for we know that looked after young people are often a troubled group, presenting with high levels of difficulties as a result of early childhood experiences, which without support can impinge on progress throughout and after care. Additionally, government figures show that children and young people in care are largely drawn from disadvantaged families (Stein, 2004). Taken together this suggests that many care experienced young people carry with them a heightened risk of non-participation, a message that provides an increased emphasis on the need for a stable and positive experience of care.

In-care

Future progress and life chances can also be shaped by young people's experiences in care. For many, care can have a positive impact, however, in some cases the care system can fall short of adequately compensating for earlier difficulties and disadvantage (SEU, 2003). In line with existing research, this study found that a number of features of the care experience were associated with poor outcomes after care. Amongst those found to have a particular impact on early career outcomes were risk behaviour, placement and education disruption and the age at leaving care.

For example, the looked after population has been shown to have a greater vulnerability to risk behaviour such as substance misuse (Newburn et al., 2002), offending (DfES, 2006b) and running away (SEU, 2002) when compared to the general youth population. Such difficulties whilst in care can increase the risk of ongoing and additional difficulties after care, including unemployment and social exclusion. This was demonstrated in the research, which found that those involved in offending were more likely to continue to offend after care, fared worse in education attainment and career outcomes and were more likely than non-offenders in the sample to be in the NEET group ($p=0.003$). Also, when compared to other young people, those who had problems with substance misuse appeared more likely to have poor career outcomes (38% and 69% respectively, $p = 0.013$).

This suggests that involvement in risk behaviour, and the personal difficulties associated with it, can at best divert and at worst prohibit young people from establishing an early foothold on the career ladder. Being relatively free of difficulties meanwhile raises the likelihood of entering and sustaining participation.

A further predictor of poor outcomes was instability whilst in care. Placement movement is a common feature of the care experience for all too many young people (Jackson, 2002) and has been associated with failing to settle post-care. Stability in care meanwhile promotes successful outcomes (Stein, 2004). The majority of young people in the current study had experienced several moves, over one third (37%) moving four or more times during their last care episode. Notably, those who were doing well in terms of career outcomes were more likely to have had fewer placement moves (p=0.039).

There was also some indication that the type of placement from which young people leave can impact on future participation. Those leaving foster care were less likely to be unemployed at baseline (p=0.046) and appeared less likely to become unemployed over time. It is likely that this reflects the trend towards higher participation in post-16 education amongst the foster care group and the practice of placing more troubled teenagers in residential care.

A further feature of the care career that has been linked to difficulties after care, and one which carries much relevance to career progress, is the extent to which looked after young people experience education difficulties and disruption. Whilst much focus has been placed on the education attainment of those in and leaving care, as discussed later, of equal importance is the problem of education disengagement. High rates of exclusion and truancy are evident within the looked after population generally (HM Inspectorate, 2001) and this was reflected within the current study. Almost two-thirds (62%) of young people had been excluded and 71% reported truancy (37% of which was persistent).

Truancy and exclusion are linked to poor education performance and have been identified as predictors of future risk behaviour such as offending, substance misuse, social exclusion and unemployment (Youth Justice Board, 2002; Hibbert et al., 1990). This resonates with our own findings that those who had experienced truancy and exclusion were more likely to be NEET a year after care (p=0.003).

On a practical level, missing out on school can result in missing out on work experience placements and on opportunities to develop confidence, interpersonal skills and a sense of achievement through academic and non-academic activities. As a consequence, these young people may be ill-prepared for post-16 participation, placing them at a disadvantage in the youth labour market.

Finally, for young people in the current study, the most significant factor of the care career in relation to participation was the age at which they left care. Almost three-quarters (73%) of those leaving aged 18 or over were active in EET compared to a third of those who left aged 16 (33%) or 17 (31%). This provides a clear message that those who leave care earlier have a higher risk of non-participation; a finding mirrored by Courtney et al. (2005)

who found that staying in care later facilitated participation in education and employment. It is likely that having time to complete their schooling, and gradual preparation for post-care living, provides young people with a breathing space in which to develop the skills and the circumstances from which to step onto the career ladder.

Post-care

Circumstances after care also influence career outcomes. Negotiating the changes and challenges involved in transitioning from care to independent adult living is a testing and complex process, regardless of earlier experiences. For many it can prove overwhelming and destabilising, particularly in the absence of consistent and effective support networks. For young people in the sample, a lack of stability after care could undermine progress across all life areas, including finding and sustaining participation in EET.

The Work Foundation's categorisation of the causes of unemployment provides a useful framework for considering the specific experiences reported by young people in the study, in relation to participation and the barriers they faced in terms of their post-care circumstances. Barriers to employment are categorised as personal (skills, confidence, circumstances and lack of career information), institutional (benefit regimes, training programme design and capacity), local (core public services, childcare and transport) and structural (lack of demand, hiring behaviour, attraction of informal economy) (Jones et al., 2004).

Personal barriers include poor education attainment, which can have an enduring impact on career opportunities. Failure to achieve educationally is a widespread and much publicised difficulty for care-experienced youth. Over half (54%) of young people in the study had no qualifications, broadly reflecting the national picture (57%) (DfESb, 2006) and highlighting the considerable disparity to the general population, where only 5% leave school without qualifications. Unsurprisingly, we found that good education performance increases employability, with all but one of those in employment in the study having achieved a good education outcome (p=0.028).[3]

Personal barriers to successful career outcomes were also located in the transitional process itself and the practicalities of post-care living. Unlike normative transitions, which happen gradually, care leavers experience a number of key transitional events at an earlier age and in a shorter space of time. Finding a home, a career and rebuilding family and social networks tend to overlap in the immediate months after leaving care (Biehal et al., 1995) and can present competing demands and challenges for those adapting to post-care living and the resulting increased adult responsibilities.

Leaving care brings with it the need for suitable post-care accommodation as few care leavers can or do return to their families. Many young people, as was the case in this study, move to semi-independent or independent living and sustaining their independent living status can be difficult on a financial, emotional and practical level. Indeed, most leave care before the age of 18 having received limited preparation for independent living (Biehal et al., 1995) and subsequently, accommodation breakdown and movement are common. A third of young people in our sample had moved home three times and one in five had experienced five moves or more. Additionally, periods of homelessness affected 35%. Those who had experienced greater post-care housing instability were more likely to be unemployed (p=0.04).

Whilst housing and career are mutually reinforcing, insecure accommodation can clearly undermine career stability and participation. Understandably perhaps, young people are more likely to give priority to more pressing needs such as homemaking, therefore for most care leavers (and those supporting them) securing and managing accommodation often takes precedence over finding a career (Dixon et al., 2006). This being so, care leavers may therefore have a delayed entry into EET participation when compared to other young people, who are more likely to establish a career path before leaving home.

Personal difficulties can also undermine the ability to find or sustain employment, education or training. As discussed earlier, care leavers may be struggling with involvement in substance misuse or offending. Our research found that having a good career outcome was associated with fewer difficulties such as offending (p<0.01) and substance misuse (p=0.05). Additionally, young people with mental health, emotional or behavioural difficulties were more likely to have a poor career outcome at follow-up (p<0.01).

Institutional barriers such as benefits regimes meanwhile, are particularly relevant to carer leavers. As we have seen, most enter the NEET group in the early years after care and are subsequently economically inactive (Broad, 1998; Dixon and Stein, 2005). Under the CLCA those below 18 receive financial support for living and housing costs from their local authority (with the exception of young parents and young disabled people). Those rising 18 are entitled to job seekers allowance and housing benefit. However, high accommodation costs and low pay for young people in work can conspire to increase the likelihood of falling into 'the benefits trap', where reliance on benefits can prove a disincentive to participation. Furthermore, rules for benefits entitlement, which require the claimant to be available for work, may prevent young people from participating in some forms of education or training.

In terms of local barriers, a lack of transport and childcare services can offer additional challenges to finding and sustaining participation. Young people commented on a lack of choice in where they were housed, which could result in them being remote from education, employment and training providers. Although care leavers are entitled to EET related costs, including travel, via their leaving care team, difficulties with distance and travel could prove a disincentive to participation. Also, whilst finding opportunities that fit around childcare responsibilities, is an issue for all parents, it is perhaps more so for those young parents, such as care leavers, who are estranged from their family networks and therefore unable to rely on informal assistance.

Structural barriers affecting care leavers' access to career opportunities include wider labour market trends affecting the workforce in general. The demand for a more skilled labour force and changes to the availability and range of options can impact upon the career trajectories of all young people. However, poor attainment amongst the care leaver group places them at a greater disadvantage in a labour market that places a high premium on academic achievement.

Finally, financial circumstances can also influence young people's participation in EET. Pay scales for young adults are often structured to reflect the norm of remaining within the family home and receiving parental support until the early twenties. Income for those in the study who were employed ranged from £40 a week to a more respectable £250 and the average for those in education and training was £53 and £59 respectively. Payments for most forms of youth participation can, therefore, be insufficient to sustain independent living. This research suggested that some young people were either deterred from participation or encouraged to participate in unsuitable educational courses rather than employment, because the high costs of their accommodation meant that, as one PA concluded, *'it doesn't pay to work'.*

Overall, these obstacles present a significant challenge to young people who may already be struggling with the responsibilities of independent living, personal difficulties or motivation. They also present a challenge to those working to support young people into participation.

Increasing the chance of success and overcoming obstacles

We have seen that participation in education, employment and training is lower for care leavers than the youth population generally and sustaining participation against a background of wider difficulties is a challenge. What are the implications for care and leaving care services? Our research highlights a number of factors that can facilitate or obstruct participation in EET and suggests ways in which young people can be assisted to overcome obstacles and maximise their potential and employability.

The findings demonstrate that leaving care later and from a stable care background, can increase the chances of both educational attainment at school, and post-16 participation in EET. Proposals to reduce placement movement and educational disruption are prominent in current policies, including the White Paper (DfES, 2007). Similarly, proposals to enable young people to remain in care longer are highlighted. Of course this requires allowing young people the option to remain in their placements, which brings with it the need for adequate placement availability and financing.

An increased focus on education and career planning whilst in care can also increase young people's potential and options within the labour market. A number of strategies exist to support the education of looked after children. The Children Act 2004 imposes a specific duty on local authorities to promote and increase the educational achievement of looked-after children, whilst measures intended to improve educational outcomes include a duty to give priority to looked-after children in the schools admissions process. However, there is also a need to strengthen the focus on careers within young people's care plans and pathway plans. This would enable an early assessment of strengths and aspirations and enable professionals to help young people address deficits in skills, abilities and motivation far sooner.

The research also suggests that services need to give greater attention to groups at higher risk of non-participation such as young people coping with emotional, mental health or behavioural problems and those involved in substance misuse or offending. As we have seen, those more troubled young people are more likely to be unemployed which can perpetuate further risk behaviour. Those with more complex needs will, therefore, require more intensive and structured support to address their immediate difficulties and facilitate post-16 participation. This was evident within the study sample with those who had multiple difficulties receiving more intensive support (p= 0.023). However, providing more intensive support to trouble young people could have consequences for service resources. Leaving care staff noted that this group often drew heavily on their time and meant that those young people considered to be doing better received less support.

Findings also highlight the need to recognise that for some young people, an early and poorly prepared move into education, employment or training can prove overly challenging and, particularly if unsuccessful, ultimately discouraging. Strategies to support participation may well need to consider a longer-term approach to facilitate a delayed or gradual arrival into the career arena. Also, given the obstacles that many care leavers encounter in making the transition into EET, it is important that they receive consistent support to overcome earlier disadvantage and on-going difficulties. It has been seen in this research that a positive experience of care based on placement stability, educational participation and support to reduce risk behaviour can make a difference to outcomes, and that the opportunity to make a gradual transition from care and achieve post-care stability can facilitate successful post-16 participation. However, even where these conditions were not readily apparent, a common feature for those making progress was the provision of consistent and focused support, whether from professionals or from friends and family.

Support to increase young people's career potential and opportunities is a key part of leaving care policy. The CLCA places a duty on local authorities to support young people, in some cases up to the age of 24, as they make the transition to independent living. This includes help with accommodation, finances, developing positive self-esteem and the ability and resources to achieve their aspirations as well as career choices. In terms of specific careers support, it was found that local authorities employed a range of measures to tackle the causes of non-participation and increase employability. Some leaving care teams in the study had engaged a member of staff with a specific remit for increasing participation. In other areas Connexions advisors were seconded to the leaving care team to work with young people in and leaving care whilst in others, multi-agency steering groups had been established to co-ordinate access to education and employment and to monitor local outcomes. Local authorities also offered a range of initiatives to increase care leavers' skills. For example, they offered workshops on basic literacy, numeracy and information technology and access to mainstream initiatives such as the New Deal. More, however, could be made of Corporate Parenting (CP) as a means of increasing career opportunities for care leavers. For example, employability schemes could be established which involve ring-fencing work experience placements or jobs within the council and guaranteeing interviews for care leavers who apply for council jobs. Although such a strategy was mentioned in some areas, it appeared to be fairly limited in scope and take-up.

Similarly, local businesses appeared to be a much under-used resource, in that none of the participating local authorities had drawn in the support of local employers to increase participation for care leavers. Through the principle of Corporate Social Responsibility (CSR) and initiatives such as Business in the Community, local businesses give a commitment to supporting vulnerable groups in the local area by providing work or sponsorship. One example is the Starting Blocks Project, which involved a voluntary agreement between a local authority and a large private company to provide a programme of supported work experience placements to care leavers. Findings from a pilot project suggest that supported work placements can offer an opportunity to develop or refresh skills, build confidence and self-esteem as well as challenge or confirm career goals and importantly, for more vulnerable young people who lack the confidence to engage in EET, provide a stepping stone to mainstream initiatives (Dixon, 2006). At a more strategic level, therefore, CP and CSR can provide important resources and opportunities for helping care leavers gain work related experience, and drive up their potential and participation.

Conclusion

The findings discussed in this paper reflect and confirm existing research and practice evidence that: many care leavers continue to face considerable challenges in finding and sustaining education, employment and training in the early years after care. Findings also highlight the association between key feature of the care and leaving care experiences and career outcomes, demonstrating that many care leavers face disadvantage as a legacy of their earlier experiences and post-care circumstances.

Recent initiatives to engage care leavers include promoting further education, both as a pathway to higher education and work and as a valuable step in its own right, alongside facilitating entry into training and work experience programmes to increase work skills and readiness. These are imperative and require proper funding and ongoing monitoring. However, despite an increase in the range of options and initiatives to increase participation, there remains a significant gap in achievement and engagement for the care leaver group when compared to their non-care peers. Factors associated with non-participation can be located within the pre-care, in-care and post-care experience. In recognising these obstacles, carers, social work professionals and leaving care services can target support more effectively.

This research concluded that having a solid foundation from which to make the transition to adulthood is most important. Factors that enable young people to maximise their career chances include identifying emotional and health needs early, addressing the causes of truancy and exclusion, and increasing education attainment for young people in and leaving care. Increasing in-care stability and, importantly, delaying the age of leaving care are also crucial. However, whilst these messages are echoed within the White Paper (DfES, 2007), they carry wider implications for the availability of care places for young adults and the retention and recruitment of foster carers more generally.

Post-16 participation cannot be addressed in isolation. Whilst much can be done to better equip and prepare looked after young people for life after care, wider structural factors can remain a challenge. Giving consideration to the type of accommodation available to young people leaving care, including the location and cost, is a crucial factor in smoothing the pathway towards participation. Adequate pay for those in EET and greater flexibility for undertaking training and work experience for those on benefits can also lead to increased and sustained participation.

Finally, holistic support after care can help young people address personal difficulties, reduce risk behaviour and secure stable accommodation, thus providing a more conducive context for embarking upon education, employment or training. It is without doubt amongst the most important factors in improving outcomes. Focused, consistent support whether from leaving care professionals, other agencies or family and friends can turn poor outcomes around and help sustain success, both in terms of career and life chances in general. These are enduring challenges. The White Paper (DFES, 2007) and the subsequent Children and Young Person's Bill provide a new and important opportunity for services to work together to meet these challenges and to enable young people in and leaving care to reach their full potential and achieve economic and general well-being after care.

Acknowledgements

The author acknowledges the contribution of members of the research team; Jim Wade, Jenny Lee and Helen Weatherly (University of York) and Sarah Byford (Institute of Psychiatry)

Notes

1. In most cases the p-value is given if the test was statistically significant (i.e. p=0.05 or less). This simply means that the probability of the result or association happening by chance is less than 5 in 100.
2. A 'good' career outcome was assigned where the young person was economically active and progress was rated as positive by the PA. If either was rated negatively, a 'poor' outcome was assigned. Young parents were not included in the outcome analysis.
3. The PAF A2 indicator of one or more GCSEs or GNVQs at any level was used as a measure of a 'good' educational outcome.

References

Banks, M., Bates, I., Breakwell, G., Bynner, J., Emler, N., Jamieson, L., and Roberts, K. (1992) *Careers and Identities*. Buckingham: Open University Press

Biehal, N., Clayden, J., Stein, M., and Wade, J. (1995) *Moving On: young people and leaving care schemes*. London: HMSO

Broad, B. (1998) *Young People Leaving Care: Life after the Children Act 1989*. London: Jessica Kingsley

Broad, B. (2003) *After the Act: Implementing the Children (Leaving Care) Act 2000*.

(De Montfort University, Children and Families Research Unit Monograph, No. 3) Leicester: De Montfort University

Bynner, J. and Parsons, S. (2002) Social exclusion and the transition from school to work: The case of young people not in education, employment or training. *Journal of Vocational Behaviour*, 60,: 289-309

Cheung, Y. and Heath, A. (1994) After care: The education and occupation of adults who have been in care'. *Oxford Review of Education*, 20, 3, 361-374

Courtney, M., Dworsky, A., Ruth, G., Keller, T., Havlicek, J., and Bost, N. (2005) *Midwest Evaluation of the Functioning of Former Foster Youth: Outcomes at age 19.* Chicago: University of Chicago, Chapin Hall Centre for Children

Department for Education and Skills (2000) *Youth Cohort Study: Education, training and employment of 16-18 year olds in England.* (Statistical Bulletin, May) London: DfES

Department for Education and Skills (2003) *Participation in Education, Training and Employment by 16 – 18 year olds in England: 2001 and 2002.* London: DfES

Department for Education and Skills (2005) *Participation in education training and employment by 16-18 year olds in England 1985 to 2003.* London: DfES

Department for Education and Skills (2006a) *Children Looked After in England (including Adoptions and Care leavers) 2005-06.* London: DfES

Department for Education and Skills (2006b) *Outcome Indicators for Looked After Children: Twelve months to 30 September 2005.* England. London: DfES

Department for Education and Skills (2006c) *Youth Cohort Study: The activities and experiences of 18 year olds: England and Wales.* London: DfES

Department for Education and Skills (2006d) *Care Matters: Transforming the lives of Children and Young People in Care.* HMSO

Department for Education and Skills (2007) *Care Matters: Time for change.* London: HMSO

Dixon, J. and Stein, M. (2005) *Leaving Care: Throughcare and aftercare in Scotland.* London: Jessica Kingsley

Dixon, J. (2006) *Pathways to Work Experience: Helping care leavers into employment. a review of the York Cares Starting Blocks Project.* York: University of York, Social Work Research and Development Unit

Dixon, J., Wade, J., Byford, S., Weatherly, H., and Lee, J. (2006) Young People Leaving Care: A study of costs and outcomes. Report to the DfES. York: University of York, Social Work Research and Development Unit

Hibbert, A., Fogelman, K. and Maoner, O. (1990) Occupational outcomes of truancy. *British Journal of Education Psychology*, 60, 1, 23-36

HM Inspectors of Schools and the Social Work Services Inspectorate (2001) *Learning with Care. The education of children looked after away from home by local authorities.* Edinburgh: Scottish Executive

Jackson, S. (2002) Promoting stability and continuity in care away from home, in D. McNeish, T. Newman, and R. Roberts *What Works for Children?* Buckingham: Open University Press

Jackson, S., Ajayi, S., and Quigley, M. (2003) *By Degrees: The first year from care to university.* London: University of London, Thomas Coram Research Unit

Jones, A., Nathan, M., and Westwood, A. (2004) *Marks and Start: Opening the door to employment?* London: The Work Foundation

Newburn, T., Ward, J., and Pearson, G. (2002) *Drug Use among Young People in Care.* Youth Citizenship and Social Change Research Briefing Paper, no.7, Autumn. Swindon: ESRC

Pinkerton, J. and McCrea, R. (1999) *Meeting the Challenge? Young people leaving care in Northern Ireland.* Aldershot: Ashgate

Social Exclusion Unit (2003) *A Better Education for Children in care,* London: Social Exclusion Unit

Social Exclusion Unit (2002) *Young Runaways.* London: Social Exclusion Unit

Stein, M. (2004) *What Works for Young People Leaving Care?* Barkingside: Barnardos

Stein, M. and Carey, K. (1986) *Leaving Care,* Oxford: Blackwell

Youth Justice Board (2002) *Summary of the MORI 2002 Youth Survey.* London: Youth Justice Board

11
Carers and looked after children: The challenges ahead

Carole Smith

Introduction:
Carers, children and the looked-after system

Chapter one of this book shows how foster care has developed from a largely informal and private enterprise to a service that is at the centre of looking after children and young people who, for various reasons and for differing periods of time, cannot live with their birth families. As a service, foster care is clearly embedded in a wider system comprising education and health services, forms of regulation and monitoring and arrangements for assessment, review and planning for looked after children. Thus, while chapter three of the Government's White Paper, *Care Matters: Time for Change* (Secretary of State for Education and Skills 2007) locates foster care in the context of care placements (Chapter three), references to the responsibilities of foster and other carers can be identified throughout proposals for improving outcomes for looked after children. For example, social workers must work with carers to 'arrange high quality early years education as part of the child's care plan' (4.10), carers must be involved in designing and delivering Personal Education Plans for looked after children (4.33), and carers should develop good links with schools, attend school parents' evenings, help children with their homework and encourage values and aspirations that support educational achievement (4.88). Carers should also encourage looked after children to engage in healthy lifestyles through attention to diet and providing support for their involvement in leisure, volunteering and sporting activities (Chapter five). Foster care will also extend beyond the responsibilities associated with caring for children and young people to providing support into young adulthood. The Government intends to pilot arrangements from 2008-09 for young people with 'familial relationships' with foster carers to remain in their placements until they are aged twenty-one. Improved training provision for carers will help them 'acquire the skills needed to help young people, including those with complex needs and disabilities, learn the practicalities of living alone' (6.33).

The emphasis in the Green Paper, *Care Matters* (Secretary of State for Education and Skills 2006) and in the subsequent White Paper, on the central role of carers in helping looked after children to achieve the five outcomes in *Every Child Matters* (Chief Secretary to the Treasury 2003) is hardly surprising. Research suggests that placement quality and stability and the skills, attitudes and commitment demonstrated by carers, significantly influence children's well being and their ability to develop into socially and economically competent adults (see research reported in Department of Health 1991; Berridge 1997; Sinclair 2005 and by Dixon, and Lipscombe and Farmer in this book). We also know that multiple placements resulting from insufficient supply, organisational requirements, stressed carers, and the sometimes difficult and challenging behaviour of looked after children and young people can threaten the quality and stability of care that is provided (Maluccio and Ainsworth, 2006; Sinclair, 2005).

Care Matters: Time for Change includes policy and legislative proposals that seek to address some of these issues within an integrated system that is designed to respond to children's educational, health care and socio-emotional needs. However, a system by its very nature, requires a logical, methodical and ordered integration of its functionally related parts (see Luhmann 1995 for a discussion of the nature and functions of social systems). This chapter will address system imperatives from two perspectives. First, attention will be given to the complex and multi-faceted nature of carers' roles and responsibilities and suggest that the Government has thus far given up, perhaps appropriately, on the struggle to systematically structure and to functionally differentiate carers' roles in relation to children's needs. This relates to practical and organisational issues. Second, from an altogether different perspective, the Government's emphasis on the relationship between carers' competencies and children's outcomes will be challenged, and it will be suggested that an alternative approach to thinking about the provision of *care* is required. This relates to moral issues associated with trust, uncertainty and experience in opposition to instrumental and functional imperatives that focus on outcomes. Designing and implementing a system of care provision that supports corporate and individual parenting, particularly for children and young people whose development has already been adversely affected, presents an extraordinary challenge to Government, managers, professional practitioners and carers. It is likely, therefore, that the system will be characterised by gaps, tensions and complexities that make it problematic to functionally differentiate its constituent parts and enable them to work smoothly together – no matter how much Government seeks to formalise, regulate and audit effective system performance. This means that some of the issues identified from research, discussed by theorists and addressed in this book, will continue to demand our attention. It is intended the discussion in this chapter will contribute something to this ongoing debate.

System imperatives: improving everyday care for children and young people

Foster and residential care

As noted above, recent policy documents make clear that the role of everyday carers is central to a child care system that aims to ameliorate the effects of children's earlier adverse experiences and enable them to develop into competent adults. In this context the Government (Secretary of State for Education and Skills 2006 and 2007) has concentrated its policy and legislative efforts on the roles of residential, foster and family and friends carers. In its White Paper, *Care Matters: Time for Change* the Government expresses its intention that all looked after children should have 'kind, understanding and committed carers' (3.1), that children and carers should be at the centre of 'the work of the wider team around the child – the social worker, health professional, teacher' (3.2) and that 'all placement decisions should be made with a view to maximising the opportunity for the child to find permanence' (3.5). If a particular placement is identified as being temporary then 'the care plan should articulate what the longer term placement option is and how the current placement will support its achievement' (3.5).

The White Paper includes proposals for more effectively enabling carers to provide permanence, engage with a child's educational and health care needs and support young people in their transition to independence. Recognising that residential care workers need to be appropriately trained to support young people, particularly in relation to education, health and relationships, the Government will 'consider with the Children's Workforce Development Council how we can best support residential workers in fulfilling this role and will look further at pathways available to residential care staff' (3.58). Additionally, the Government intends to fund a pilot programme to evaluate the effectiveness of social pedagogy in residential care with a particular focus on how group living might provide supportive relationships and developmental opportunities for young people (3.59). However, these seem to be the only identified measures to improve individual caring in residential settings and remaining Government proposals concern monitoring and regulating provider performance against the National Minimum Standards for residential care (3.61) and constraining local authorities' discretion to place children outside their areas (3.71/3.72).

Foster care attracts somewhat more detailed consideration in the White Paper and developing foster carers' knowledge and skills in high on the policy agenda. The Foster Care Training, Support and Development Standards identified by the Children's Workforce Development Council 'describe the skills and competencies that all foster carers should be able to demonstrate' (3.29). The Government intends to incorporate the training and development standards into its revision of the National Minimum Standards for fostering services so that inspections of foster care providers will be able to monitor their performance in enabling carers to meet the required standards. The standards will contribute to 'an agreed quality framework to underpin the approvals system for foster carers' (3.31) and this framework for assessing the competencies of carers 'will set out clearly the roles which carers are expected to fulfil and the skills which they need to develop' (3.32). At the same time, the framework will clarify providers' responsibilities for ensuring appropriate training and support and will provide greater consistency in assessing the competence and skills of foster carers. The Government also intends to contribute to skills development in foster care by rolling out the *Fostering Changes Programme* which advises foster carers about positive parenting techniques to manage difficult and challenging behaviour (3.34) and it will provide guidance to foster carers on the provision of sex and relationship education to young people (3.35). Against this backdrop of formally identifying the training and required competencies of foster carers, the Government will establish systems for transferring information about their qualifications and skills between foster care providers (3.36/3.37). Although the Government is unwilling to impose particular training or funding requirements on foster care providers it will require all fostering services to 'publish details of their payment structures for foster carers, in relation to the nature of the task being undertaken and the level of training required' (3.42). In order to enhance the recruitment of foster carers, the Government will extend the Independent Review Mechanism currently operating for adoption applicants to prospective foster carers whose applications are rejected (3.38) and it will support national and local recruitment campaigns (3.44).

Kinship Care

Support and care provided by family and friends is recognised by the Government as an underdeveloped resource for children and young people who would otherwise be looked after, who are already looked after or who are placed from care. Research evidence is equivocal about the relative stability and benefits of kinship care compared to placements with non-related foster carers (see research reported in Sinclair, 2005; Maluccio and Ainsworth, 2006; Colten *et al* 2008; and Broad in this book). The 'value added' contribution of kinship carers lies in their enhanced sense of commitment, their local availability, familiarity and already established relationships between carers and children and opportunities for contact with wider family and friends. However, making this form of care the preferred option for children and young people who are already, or who are likely to become looked after, is not straightforward. It is not, as Sinclair (2005, p.44) points out a 'free lunch'. Nevertheless, the Government intends to include in the revised Children Act 1989 Guidance a requirement that during a core assessment, 'consideration is given to the willingness and capacity of the wider family to care for the child on a shorter or longer term basis' (2.40) and it will ensure that 'relatives and friends are, as far as possible, considered in all cases as potential carers as part of the care plan lodged with the court at the outset of care proceedings' (Secretary of State for Education and Skills 2007: 2.38).

The Government recognises that kinship carers have particular characteristics, which differentiate them and their support needs from non-relative foster carers. Overall, they are likely to be more financially and educationally disadvantaged, older and in poorer health. In many cases they may be struggling to manage the behaviour of children and young people living with them, and to cope with conflict within the extended family. They also tend to be less well supported by social workers and less well trained and remunerated by local authorities. With this in mind, the Government's White Paper intends that family and friends carers will receive appropriate support and recognition through 'a new framework for family and friends care which will set out the expectations of an effective service to enable children to remain within their wider families and communities' (2.36). This framework will address variations in the use of family and friends placements across local authorities, absent or inconsistent local policies determining services for these carers, lack of transparency about available entitlements and services and the suitability of the approval process for family and friends (2.37). In terms of legal status and associated financial support, the Government will legislate to enable relative carers to apply for a residence order if the child has lived continuously with them for a minimum of one year immediately preceding the application (as is the case for local authority foster carers) and to raise the age at which a residence order automatically ends from sixteen to eighteen (2.43; 2.47). The Government notes that it will consider making timescales for enabling relative carers to apply for special guardianship and adoption orders consistent with this change (2.44). For those carers who already have a residence order, the Government will ensure that parental responsibility and any residence order allowance will continue until the child is eighteen.

Everyday care: radical proposals for change?

Proposals in the White Paper for improving the quality and stability of residential and foster care represent a much diluted version of Government thinking in the preceding Green Paper (Secretary of State for Education and Skills 2006). The Green Paper indicated Government's preference for 'developing a national tiered model of placement types underpinned by a national qualifications framework for foster and residential carers' (4.30). The tiered model would have reflected the level of sophistication in carers' skills and offered career progression through the development of higher level skills and movement up through the tiers. Skills development would be based on identified competencies in the context of a new framework of skills and qualifications, including a new Foundation Degree and the possibility of progressing to a degree level qualification. There would be a mandatory registration scheme for foster carers (4.34). However, respondents to the Green Paper consultation anticipated significant difficulties associated with the tiered model (Department for Education and Skills 2007: 4.9-4.13; Social Care Institute for Excellence 2007, p.20). A tiered model as the basis for individually matching children's needs and carers' skills was not pursued in the White Paper. The proposal for a national qualifications framework has been replaced by devolving responsibility to providers of fostering services for ensuring that carers are able to demonstrate centrally specified skills and competencies. It seems that the mandatory registration scheme for foster carers has now disappeared from the policy agenda. The decision in the White Paper to leave training and funding arrangements to fostering service providers must come as a disappointment to those who have lobbied for a 'professional' foster care service that, as Hutchinson (2003, p.8) suggests, 'offers a career structure to carers, with all that that involves in terms of training, support, remuneration and working conditions' (see also, National Foster Care Association 1997 and a critical discussion of 'professionalization' by Wilson and Evetts 2006; and by Kirton in this book).

Residential care workers have little more than a promise that the Children's Workforce Development Council will consider how best to support them in their role, and a planned pilot to evaluate the effectiveness of social pedagogy in residential care. The White Paper's intention to develop kinship care seem to depend largely on monitoring and regulating local authorities' performance in this context and on tinkering with legal requirements and the duration of a residence order. However, the Government intends to pilot Regional Commissioning Units for foster and residential care to increase opportunities for greater placement choice such that 'a menu of appropriate placements, tailored to meet the needs of the child, is available when the placement decision is being made' (Secretary of State for Education and Skills 2007: 3.16). Pooling available placement resources may increase choice, but this is only likely to be the case if the overall provision of foster and residential care placements can be increased. The White Paper will 'impose a statutory duty on local authorities to secure a sufficient and diverse provision of quality placements within their local area' (3.13). As in other areas of health and social care, the Government seems to think that imposing *duties* on service providers and establishing a commissioning model of service provision will sort out previously intractable and complex issues associated with supply, demand and choice.

System imperatives: integration and functional differentiation of everyday care

Commenting on the high financial expenditure on placements for looked after children, the Government remarks that outcomes are still 'unacceptably low' and that 'the system does not yet do enough to address the harm that children have suffered before entering care' (Secretary for Education and Skills 2007: 1.33). Clearly, residential and foster carers make a significant contribution to system effectiveness but their integration into the system has remained marginal in some respects and their functional differentiation has been piecemeal and incoherent. In response to criticism that residential and foster carers remain relatively poorly equipped in terms of knowledge, skills and status to contribute to better outcomes for children, the Green and White Papers have established clear expectations about their roles. They are charged with responsibilities in relation to children's social and emotional development, educational progress and maintaining healthy lifestyles, as integral members of the child care team. Their ability to meet these expectations will apparently be assured by a training and development framework based on the achievement and demonstration of competencies that are necessary for effective role performance. Although the Government has introduced national minimum financial allowances for foster carers based on the ages of looked after children, it is estimated that approximately 40% of carers do not receive any fees in addition to payments intended to cover their basic costs (Swain 2007). These arrangements are a long way from a professional model of fostering where foster carers would be fully integrated members of the child care team by virtue of their skills and remuneration. Respect for their contribution would be both symbolised by these features of their 'work' and would be appropriately given by professional practitioners in response to their status.

The growth of independent fostering providers, discussed by Sellick in this book, has also created a fostering workforce that enjoys many advantages, which are also sought on behalf of local authority foster carers – generous remuneration, training and support that appropriately reflect the challenges of caring for looked after children and young people. Statistical information from the Department for Children, Schools and Families (DCSF) indicates that approximately 16% of children looked after at the end of March 2007 were placed by independent fostering providers operating in the voluntary and private sectors (DCSF 2007). The Government clearly recognises the contribution of this sector: its operations sit readily with policies across health and social care that seek to extend the supply and choice of services and to drive up standards, through a commissioning strategy. From initially suspicious and hostile relationships between local authorities and private fostering agencies (Association of Directors of Social Services 1997) and a perception that independent providers fell outside the child care system, mutual dependence and Government sponsorship have latterly supported closer co-operation at the level of service provision. However, despite the growing use of independent sector placements for looked after children, their integration into the child care system arguably depends on a framework of regulation and shared market interests. The Office for Standards in Education, Children's Services and Skills is responsible for inspecting and regulating independent sector and local authority fostering services against National Minimum Standards. The White Paper (Secretary of State for Education and Skills 2007: 3.31) notes that, in future it will assess how far fostering providers are ensuring that foster carers meet new skills and competencies standards. The Government intends that local authorities should obtain aggregated information about children in need and in care from the integrated children's system to inform a commissioning strategy for service provision. To assist local authorities to develop commissioning for fostering and residential placements, the Government will establish Regional Commissioning Unit pilots, issue guidance on managing local placement markets, develop National Occupational Standards for service commissioners and support the development of a standardised national contract for residential care (Secretary of State for Education and Skills 2007: 3.16-3.23).

Kinship care arguably has a tangential relationship to the care system, unless kinship carers are also foster carers. It has been recognised that kinship carers' social, educational and economic characteristics tend to differentiate them from non-relative foster carers and that they are treated less favourably in terms of training, support and financial help by local authorities. Most kinship carers will either provide care informally or with the legal protection of a residence order, or possibly a special guardianship order, under sections 8-14 and 14A (as amended) of the Children Act 1989 respectively. Recent legal challenges to local authorities' unwillingness to pay equitable financial allowances to kinship carers have resulted in judicial support for payments based on a child's needs rather than on the particular relationship with their carers (see for example, *R [on application of L and others] v Manchester City Council* and *R [on application R and another] v Manchester City Council* [2001] EWHC). Kirton in this book also comments on the distinctive nature of kinship care, most notably its focus on 'continuity, familiarity, attachment and identity' – attitudes and relationships that promote care rather than skills and competencies that promote outcomes. He also suggests that many kinship carers would not be approved to care for unrelated children and that they would be unlikely to view themselves as providing a professional service with all that this involves in terms of training and participation in the care system. Kinship carers are thus unlikely members of an integrated care system and stand outside the corporate parenting project.

A system requires that its component parts are integrated into the whole system in relation to their shared characteristics, their functional contribution towards overall performance, their distinctiveness from other systems, a common discourse and a shared orientation towards system tasks. While care provided by local authorities, family and friends and the independent sector may be oriented towards the needs of looked after children and young people, their motivation, market orientation, professional aspirations, relative status and power and effective performance, all militate against system integration. Furthermore, the complexity of children and young people's needs and the development of differentiated placement schemes in response to these, make system integration more problematic. The particular characteristics and expectations of kinship care and the market differentiation of independent sector care introduce further tensions in relation to achieving an integrated model of service delivery. In structural and organisational terms the Government has attempted to reinforce integrated system working through, for example, requiring local authorities to establish Children's Trusts (Chief Secretary to the Treasury 2003) with associated multidisciplinary assessment and intervention. On the other hand, however, the Government has been inclined to contribute to disintegration through its plans to establish autonomous Social Care Practices as independent sector social work providers (Secretary of State for Education and Skills, 2006: 3.16-3.29). Consultation responses were mixed on this proposal and included some serious doubts about the consequences and likely effectiveness of Social Care Practices. Nevertheless, the Government intends to press ahead with 'establishing a variety of two-year pilots across a diverse range of local authorities' for what will now be called Social *Work Practices* (Secretary of State for Education and Skills 2007: 7.18-7.24). All of this suggests the existence of numerous related systems for delivering placement and other services to looked after children and young people: these services are differentiated functionally, sometimes structurally and, in relation to their resources, have relative autonomy and status. It also raises several issues about Government policy. First, the policy drive to integrate services into a single system around the child introduces tensions and difficulties for managers and practitioners. Second, structural and organisational integration of functionally differentiated parts cannot always be accommodated within a single system. The major challenge thus changes from attempting to incorporate all service provision into a single system, to understanding and facilitating relationships between different systems which are working towards a common goal. Third, the Government should be extremely careful about promoting further disintegration, thinking that it can govern relationships between diverse systems simply through legislation and regulation. Finally, a much more sophisticated understanding of how functionally differentiated systems might work together is required. Reliance on an oversimplified and apparently unproblematic concept of *the system* to improve outcomes for looked after children and young people is inadequate.

Systems, outcomes and the nature of care

Systems and outcomes: children and young people

The discussion above has concentrated on Government proposals, which are designed to achieve a more effective relationship between system performance and desirable outcomes (targets) for looked after children and young people. It engages with the Government's own discourse, which incorporates a reliance on organisational and structural features of service provision, carers and professional practitioners' competence to carry out relevant tasks, National Standards against which performance is assessed, the regulation of caring activities and outcomes as an end measure of effective system performance. In this section the nature of this discourse is challenged and some alternative ways of understanding the experiences of carers and looked after children are suggested.

In this book, Harlow and Frost suggest that the Government's outcome measures are crude and simplistic since they 'detach young people from their backgrounds', fail to incorporate any awareness of pre-care difficulties and assess educational and social performance at a particular point beyond which young people may mature and develop into competent adults. It is argued here, however, that Government outcome measures are flawed in a much more profound way, since they neglect how children and young people *experience* relationships, learning opportunities and social expectations, as the basis for growing confidence, feeling safe, a tentative willingness to trust significant others, enhanced concentration and the ability to learn. Children and young people may not perform at the same level as their non-looked after peers, but they may experience a greater sense of wellbeing and security than they did in their pre-care situations. In his research summary, Sinclair (2005, pp.50-52) identifies common themes arising from the views of children and young people in foster care. They wanted to be 'normal' and not to be differentiated from their peers because of administrative and legal requirements of the care system; they wanted a sense of belonging and to be 'loved, listened to and encouraged' within their foster families; they wanted their wishes and feelings about contact with their birth families to be understood and respected; they emphasised the importance of carers and professional practitioners listening to their views about a range of matters; and they aspired, with the help of their foster carers, 'to get their lives in order' and to make use of opportunities that had previously been unavailable to them. 'Children wanted relationships and they needed them... they valued the love and concern of their foster carers' (Sinclair, 2005, p.53). Similarly, conversations with fifty-nine adopted children included in Smith and Logan's (2004) research on post-adoption contact displayed two major themes. The majority of children (90%) felt very positive about adoption because they felt *safe* and because they felt *secure and loved*. As one twelve year old child said:

> I'm happy. This is because I know I am safe and nothing bad is going to happen. Also, I feel really happy because I know that people really do love me and care for me and I don't have to move around anymore (Smith and Logan, 2004, p.133).

The Government recognises the importance of these qualitative features of children's experience. In *Care Matters: Time for Change* (Secretary of State for Education and Skills 2007: 1.15) it refers to 'the close, loving relationships that enable children to feel secure and to grow and develop' and it points to the lack of such relationships as diminishing children's willingness and ability to trust 'carers and adults around them'. Government also seems to acknowledge that children's individual experiences cannot be entirely governed by the system that sets out to improve them. It states 'children and young people told us very clearly...that while a focus on systems, placement and workforce is important, what is also crucial to them is that they are not singled out in front of their peers as being in care' (Secretary of State for Education and Skills 2007: 3.7). However, the sense of wellbeing that children and young people gain from all of these experiential aspects of their lives does not appear to be viewed by Government as a moral good in itself. It is only considered as an instrumental good in the sense that it contributes to valued outcomes and serves to produce competent citizens. The Government says:

> Children in care deserve the best experiences in life, from excellent parenting and education to a wide range of opportunities to develop their talents and skills, in order to have an enjoyable childhood and successful adult life. Stable placements, emotional wellbeing and support for transitions are essential elements of this success but children and young people will only achieve their potential through the ambition and high expectations of all those involved in their lives (Secretary of State for Education and Skills, 2007: 1.1).

While an enjoyable childhood is mentioned here, 'stable placements, emotional wellbeing and support for transitions' are emphasised as contributing to a 'successful adult life'. It is unlikely that there would be a quarrel with a policy 'vision' that seeks to improve the life chances of looked after children and young people though providing better opportunities for their social, emotional and educational development. However, the Government seems unwilling to accept that improvements might more appropriately be assessed as *relative* to children's previous experiences rather than with reference to objectively specified outcomes. Its instrumentally driven policy imperatives cannot attribute value to the experiential quality of children's everyday lives unless this results in their better functioning as citizens and by virtue of this serves to demonstrate effective system performance.

Systems and outcomes: permanent placements

In order to enjoy their childhood and to mature into competent adults, children and young people need the opportunity to develop trusting relationships with their everyday carers and with others. These trusting relationships act as a springboard for enhancing confidence, self-esteem and a sense of mastery over past fears and anxieties. They also encourage optimistic possibilities for the future. However, research has repeatedly pointed to difficulties inherent in providing the kind of stable and secure placements that allow trusting relationships to develop. Sinclair (2005, p.34) suggests that for those looked after children aged between five and sixteen for whom long term fostering might be considered appropriate, 'there were the problems of breakdowns which, depending on the child's age when placement was made, probably affected about half the children who were supposed to be placed long term'. Bullock *et al* (2006) estimate that, of the total number of children recorded as being looked after at the end of March 2004, approximately 20,000 children and young people had been in care for four years or more and could therefore be regarded as 'growing up in care'. However, National Statistics (DES 2007) show that at the end of March 2007, only 66% of children who had been looked after continuously for at least two and a half years had been in the same placement for at least two years or had been placed for adoption. This indicates that there are a significant number of children in 'long term' care, many of whom will have experienced placement change or may do so as their 'looked after' status extends beyond the Government's measurement period of two years. Their experience of placement stability falls short of the Government's Public Service Agreement target that by 2008, 80% of such children should have remained in the same placement for at least two years.

Government policy is committed to achieving permanent placements for children and young people whether children live at home, in (substitute) family or residential care and whether they are looked after throughout their childhood or for relatively short periods of time. However, in this context the dangers of relying on targets, outcomes and oversimplification are only too apparent. In its research review, the Department of Health (1991) points to evidence that some children's placements at home lasted, but subjected children to further neglect and abuse. While some adolescents' placements disrupted, these had provided a positive experience for the young people concerned. Quoting Thoburn (1990) the Department (1991, p.66) says 'it is not enough to establish that the youngster remained in placement if it is not clear that permanence in any particular case has indeed contributed to wellbeing'. Sinclair's (2005) later summary of research completed or published since 1998 also indicates the uncertain futures and further harm, which are not infrequently experienced by looked after children who return home. Thankfully, the Government has decided not to introduce a numerical target to regulate the size of the care population, although it had been minded to do so (Secretary of State for Education and Skills 2007: 2.5). Beek and Schofield (2004, p.19) echo concerns about placement quality in their follow-up research on the progress of children in 'long-term' foster care. They note:

> Placement stability is only one aspect to consider when assessing outcomes for children in foster care. A placement might endure for many years but not provide an environment in which a child can thrive and flourish (Beek and Schofield 2004, p.19).

The Government's Public Service Agreement target to monitor placement stability neglects these complex and qualitative elements of children's experience while they are being looked after. Ensuring that permanence contributes to children's wellbeing requires three major factors. First, carers should feel sufficiently secure and supported to discuss placement quality with their social workers if they and the children for whom they are caring are unhappy or distressed. Second, social workers should have the time, knowledge and understanding to assess placement quality and the discretion to respond appropriately if placements are damaging for children. Third, in circumstances where children must move, social workers and carers should work together with children so that the situation is managed honestly and constructively. A placement move does not have to be inevitably clouded by a sense of chaos and failure. Unfortunately, if foster carers are focused on demonstrating their competence and social workers are concerned with meeting targets, these conditions may be difficult to achieve.

Systems and outcomes: skills, competence and caring relationships

The Government's intention to identify training, skills and competencies for foster carers and to link these to new National Minimum Standards for fostering services, 'setting out clearly the roles that carers are expected to fulfil and the skills which they need to develop' (Secretary for Education and Skills 2007: 3.32) has been discussed above. The efforts to equip carers with necessary knowledge and skills should not be dismissed nor should research findings that suggest training appears to have little impact on placement outcomes be accepted uncritically (Sinclair 2005, p.83). However, something about the qualities of carers that contribute to stable and good quality placements, and therefore to the well being of children and young people, are known. Placement stability tends to be associated with carers who are 'warm, encouraging, clear over expectations', who join in leisure activities with their foster children, who show empathy and who are sensitive to children's emotional needs (research reported in Sinclair 2005, p.80). Bearing in mind those many other factors that affect placement stability (children's age on placement, behavioural difficulties, children's attitudes to the placement, their contact with birth families) and carers' wishes to be provided with adequate remuneration, support, information and respect, Sinclair (2005, p.126) concludes:

> Foster carers who are kind, firm and slow to take offence are likely to have better results than others who embody these antique virtues to a less marked degree.

Beek and Schofield (2004, p.266) similarly comment about foster carers in their study, that their sensitivity, care, concern and ability to 'promote reflective capacity, self-esteem, autonomy and family membership' enabled them to facilitate progress for many troubled children. Clearly we have to be careful here since children and young people will need different things from being looked after, depending on their ages on entering care, plans for permanence and the way in which their previous experiences have impacted on their development and behaviour. For some young people with challenging behaviour Multi-dimensional Treatment Foster Care may be appropriate and the Government is considering rolling out knowledge from this pilot programme to similar schemes for younger children (Secretary of State for Education and Skills 2007: 3.41). Young people entering care later will need stable relationships with carers who can provide preparation and ongoing support as they move on to independence. So, carers will require different kinds of knowledge and skills depending on their role. However, carers' qualities of kindness, firmness, commitment and sensitivity are arguably relevant for all children and young people. Where children need long-term parenting until adulthood Bullock et al (2006, p.15) point to the importance of carers' qualities over their demonstrable competencies:

> This has important implications for helping separated children as the personal qualities of carers become more important as a first requirement in the selection of placements than their skills or training, with the latter building on the former rather than the reverse.

Frost's (1995) discussion of care as the vigil and the gift is relevant here. He describes care as the vigil as being embedded in a discourse that centralises knowledge, power and surveillance in relations between carers and clients such that the latter are 'disciplined' by caring interventions and their functioning rendered acceptable by caring professionals. Likening this distinction to Cixous' (1986) dichotomy between the 'gift' and the 'proper' Frost suggests that the former encourages carers to ask questions like 'here's some space for you...go for it...get on with it...I have trust and confidence in you...what can I give you to help you achieve?'. He argues that this perspective on care 'enables and empowers, it allows the recipient of the gift to become other, to establish a new subjectivity' (p. 117). The 'proper', like the vigil, however, is a discourse of discipline, where the relationship between carer and recipient is directed at achieving the latter's change towards some desired state. Care as the gift is characterised by such features as generosity, trust benevolence, love, patience and commitment, while care as vigil is based on the application of codified knowledge, authority, surveillance and 'disciplining' the unruly subject. Care as the vigil is closely associated with the professionalization of care. For example, Inglesby (1992) argues in the context of nursing, that if a candidate at interview is asked why they have chosen nursing as a career, replying that they want to help people has become an incorrect answer. References to social obligation, professional relationships, career mobility and academic and emotional gratification are likely to win greater approval. Inglesby (1992) suggests:

> The value upon care remains high, but care is no longer 'tender' and 'loving', it is a specifiable commodity...A nurse no longer has a vocation; she has a profession. She is no longer dedicated; she is professional. She is no longer moral; she is accountable.

It is not too great a leap from this discussion to social policy that aims to internally and externally 'discipline' children and young people into becoming effectively functioning citizens, to ensure surveillance of their progress towards this end and to equip carers with the necessary knowledge, skills and competencies to provide the vigil of care.

The above resistance to Government policy is not that care as vigil is entirely inappropriate; children and young people are likely to lead thoroughly miserable, unproductive and possibly dangerous lives if they cannot form trusting relationships with others, develop a sense of confidence and self-esteem, feel part of society and engage with the labour market. The quarrel with the Government is that its policy rests *entirely* on a discourse of care as vigil and pays scant attention to those qualities that characterise care as gift - qualities that we know are important to children and young people and that enable them to thrive. The practical implications of this discussion are threefold. First, practitioners should think more clearly about the balance between vigil and gift that is required in relation to children's needs. While all children and young people will need their carers to have personal qualities associated with care as gift, some will benefit from the kind of knowledge, skills and competencies that are geared towards management, containment and change – care as vigil. Second, the recruitment of carers should be as much concerned about their attitudes of generosity, compassion, care and concern as it is about their demonstration of skills and competence. Understanding carers' personal qualities, motivation and attributes will help practitioners to identify and develop their potential for different roles in relation to caring for children and young people. Third, Government should be aware that its insistence on identifying skills and competencies may fail to acknowledge and support those very qualities of care that are valued by children and young people.

Conclusion

Much has been written about systems in this concluding chapter. Social systems by their very nature are abstract in the sense that they are comprised of formal arrangements, which govern the integration of their functioning parts. Insofar as systems are concerned with content (services, human and financial resources and structural factors relating to service delivery), they refer to roles, categories and descriptive typologies. Thus, for example, Teubner (1988; 1993) argues in relation to law as a social system, that real flesh and blood people are not relevant to understanding law's operations at a systemic level. They are constructed as 'semantic artefacts' by a legal discourse that produces its own meaning and mode of communication. Specific cases involving real people should not, therefore, be confused in a systemic sense with legal representations – 'role bundles' and 'character masks' that enable us to understand and describe the system's operations. In much the same way, Giddens (1990; 1991) argues that abstract systems are disembedded from the particularities of local time and space. They do not operate at the level of specific decisions about, for example, planning for a particular child, identifying their needs, choosing a placement or the complex interactions between children and their carers or between children and their social workers. At a systems level we are more likely to be describing and discussing the *organisation* of fostering and other services for children and the *types* of care that have been developed to respond to *categories* of need. This enables the identification different systems across time and space (see for example, the international and cross-cultural analysis of family foster care by Colton *et al* 2008). Systems are instrumentally designed to achieve identified ends and their relative effectiveness can be monitored and calculated. Moral considerations concerning such qualities as trustworthiness, generosity, compassion and care are extrinsic to abstract systems.

In a similar way, research that informs evidence based practice is concerned with describing what works in particular contexts. What kind of factors associated with children, their birth families and carers might predict, for example, placement stability and what kind of pre-care and in care experiences and individual characteristics might influence outcomes for children and young people? Research of this kind is interested in identifying relationships between variables relating to populations of children, carers and birth families and/or types of intervention, training, support or whatever the focus of research might be. The important point to note, however, is that like system outcomes research, it organises its subjects and data by reference to typologies, categories, replication and its ability to predict outcomes within relative margins of confidence. It thus provides an indication of the outcomes we might expect to see under specified conditions. Sinclair (2005, p.24) notes that labelling and classification inherent in outcome research may mean that children come to be seen 'in ways they do not recognise, discussed in terms they would not accept and treated as members of a difficult group rather than as individuals in their own right' and that these organising activities commonly appear to 'treat individuals as objects'. Predictive generalisations depend on research findings for the population under study and while they may indicate a relationship between outcomes and other variables, 'research can never produce an exact answer about the degree of risk of a particular placement for an individual child because the interplay of factors which determine success or failure will be unique in each case' (Department of Health 1991, p.65). Commenting on research methodologies used to investigate sibling relationships, Mullender (1999, p.11) makes a similar point when she cautions that 'struggling even to integrate general trends it [research] does not have the capacity to predict anything about any individual child'.

Insofar as they are about outcomes, research studies and social systems share a focus on instrumentality, calculation, organisation, classification and effectiveness. They are designed to support confidence in expert knowledge and interventions (Smith 2001; 2005) and they are unable to penetrate the moral world of trust and relationships where professional practitioners must make morally loaded decisions about vulnerable children and young people. Social policy of the kind that has been discussed throughout this book also shares these features of research studies and social systems. Policy is not intended to operate at the level of messy relationships, painful experiences and morally complex decisions – these are challenges for practice. However, policy develops systems for service provision and delivery and establishes arrangements for monitoring, inspecting and measuring system performance. It also informs a particular epistemological (outcomes) approach to commissioning research that is intended to improve system performance through the application of relevant knowledge. It is not suggested here that services to families and children should be provided without the organising principles of policy, social systems and relevant knowledge about 'what works' – that would be nonsense. However, there is an issue, frequently unrecognised and unchallenged, about the way in which Government policy fails to acknowledge and support complex and morally charged encounters between social workers, carers and service users where uncertainty requires acute investigative, analytical, communicative, relational and observational skills for making assessments and decisions in *individual* cases. As indicated above, relationships with carers based on care, concern, sensitivity, generosity and commitment are also vital for the well being and positive outcomes of looked after children and young people.

So, one of the major challenges for Government is to consider how an infrastructure of services and expectations that reflects a concern with these moral issues relating to service delivery might be built. For example, as well as concentrating on arming (substitute) carers with specified knowledge, skills and competencies and implementing systems to ensure they are performing up to standard, should we ask - how might carers be recruited, prepared and supported to use their intuitive, reflective and caring qualities to provide a better experience for children and young people? Instead of piloting independent Social Work Practices, should we ask - how might we understand ways in which social work students could be better educated and prepared for practice, encouraged to develop trusting relationships with service users and supported in making morally complex decisions? The Social Care Institute for Excellence (SCIE) (2007, p.17) charges Government policy with creating those very conditions that have led it to favour establishing Social Work Practices:

The argument that the practices could cut loose from local authority bureaucracy ignores the fact that much of the procedural complexity stems from central government's requirements for safeguarding, consistent decision making, audit trails and protection of public funds, and these requirements would presumably also need to be met by these practices.

Or, as contributors to SCIE's expert seminar on *Care Matters: Time for Change* suggest, 'stop reorganising – think less about structures, more about how to promote creativity in practice and provision'. Stancombe and White (1998, p.595) argue that helping is a 'practical-moral affair, which cannot be approached as if rational-technical answers existed'. If Government could be persuaded to extend its 'vision' in a rather different direction, it might be able to see and to respond to those issues associated with helping as a 'practical-moral affair'. Its current policy discourse only serves to make such issues invisible to the detriment of professional practitioners and service users.

References

Association of Directors of Social Services (1997) *The Foster Care Market: A National Perspective*, London: ADSS

Beek, M. and Schofield, G. (2004) *Providing a Secure Base in Long-Term Foster Care*, London: British Agencies for Adoption and Fostering

Berridge, D. (1997) *Foster Care: A Research Review*, London: The Stationery Office

Bullock, R., Courtney, M., Parker, R., Sinclair, I., and Thoburn, J. (2006) Can the corporate state parent? *Adoption and Fostering*, 30, 4, 6-19

Chief Secretary to the Treasury (2003) *Every Child Matters*, London: The Stationery Office

Cixous, H. (1986) 'Sorties' in Cixous, H. and Clement, C. *The Newly Born Woman*. Manchester: Manchester University Press

Colton, M., Roberts, S. and Williams, M. (2008) 'The recruitment and retention of family foster carers: an international and cross-cultural analysis' *British Journal* of *Social Work*, 38, 5, 865-884

Department for Education and Skills (2007) *Care Matters: Consultation responses*, London: DFES

Department for Children, Schools and Families (DCSF) (2007) *National Statistics: Children Looked After in England, Year Ending 31 March 2007*

Department of Health (1991) *Patterns and Outcomes in Child Placement*, London: HMSO

Frost, N. (1995) 'Postmodern perspectives on care: the vigil and the gift', *Critical Social Policy*, 15,107-125

Giddens, A. (1990) *The Consequences of Modernity*. Cambridge: Polity Press

Giddens, A. (1991) *Modernity and Self-Identity*. Cambridge; Polity Press

Hutchinson, B. (2003) Skills protect: Towards a professional foster care service. *Adoption and Fostering* 27, 3, 8-13

Inglesby, E. (1992) Values and philosophy of nursing: The dynamic of change. in M. Jolley, M and G. Brykczynska, G. (Eds.) *Nursing Care: The challenge to change*. London: Edward Arnold

Luhmann, N. (1995) *Social Systems*, Stanford, CA: Stanford University Press

Maluccio, A. and Ainsworth, F. (2006) Family foster care: development or decline?*Adoption and Fostering* 30, 4, 20-25

Mullender, A. (1999) *We are Family: Sibling relationships in placement and beyond*. London: British Agencies for Adoption ad Fostering

National Foster Care Association (1997) *Foster Care in Crisis: A Call to professionalise the forgotten service*. London: NFCA

Secretary of State for Education and Skills (2006) *Care Matters: Transforming the lives of children and young people in care*. (Green Paper), London: The Stationery Office

Secretary of State for Education and Skills (2007) *Care Matters: Time for change*. (White Paper), London: The Stationery Office

Sinclair, I. (2005) *Fostering Now: Messages from research*. London: Jessica Kingsley

Smith, C. (2001) Trust and confidence; possibilities for social work in high modernity. *British Journal of Social Work*, 31, 287-305

Smith, C. (2005) Understanding trust and confidence: Two paradigms and their significance for health and social care. *Journal of Applied Philosophy*, 22, 3), 299-316

Smith, C. And Logan, J. (2004) *After Adoption: Direct contact and relationships*. London: Routledge

Social Care Institute for Excellence (2007) *Consultation Response – Green Paper: Care Matters*, London: SCIE

Stancombe, J. and White, S. (1998) 'Psychotherapy without foundations? Hermaneutics, discourse and the end of certainty', *Theory and Psychology*, 8(5), 579-599

Swain, V. (2007) *Can't Afford to Foster: A Survey of fee payments to foster carers*. London: Fostering Network

Teubner, G. (1988) Enterprise, corporatism: New industrial policy and the essence of the legal person. *American Journal of Comparative Law*, 36, 130-155

Teubner, G. (1993) *Law as an Autopoietic System*. Oxford; Oxford University Press

Thoburn, J. (1990) *Success and Failure in Permanent Family Placement*. Avebury

Wilson, K. and Evetts, J. (2006) The professionalization of foster care. *Adoption and Fostering*, 30, 1, 39-47

Index

Lightning Source UK Ltd.
Milton Keynes UK
UKOW041902070612

194032UK00004B/31/P